OPTIONS TRADING:

QUICK STARTERS GUIDE TO START

OPTIONS TRADING

Andrew Johnson

© 2017

Sign Up & Join <u>Andrew Johnson's Mailing List!</u>

*EXCLUSIVE UPDATES

*FREE BOOKS

*NEW REALEASE ANNOUCEMENTS BEFORE ANYONE ELSE GETS THEM

*DISCOUNTS

*GIVEAWAYS

FOR NOTIFACTIONS OF MY *NEW RELEASES* :

Never miss my next FREE PROMO, my next NEW RELEASE or a GIVEAWAY!

THIS COLLECTION INCLUDES THE FOLLOWING BOOKS:

Options Trading: A Beginners Guide to Option Trading Unlocking the Secrets of Option Trading

AND

Options Trading:The Ultimate Guide to Options Trading Uncovering Options Trading Profit Making Secrets

AND

Options Trading: Strategies on How to Excel at Options Trading

TABLE OF CONTENTS

OPTIONS TRADING: A BEGINNERS GUIDE TO OPTION TRADING UNLOCKING THE SECRETS OF OPTION TRADING

DESCRIPTION

Trading, in general, can be confusing. Options trading can be even more confusing. This is especially true if you don't know what you are doing or if you have never dealt with trading in the past.

Just because you're a beginner, though, doesn't mean that you have to stay that way. When you read this book, you will be able to learn all of the basics that you need to help make your options trading career more successful. I can't guarantee that you will make money from options trading, but I can guarantee that this book will provide you with the tools that you need to start making money.

As you are reading through the chapters, think of the different ways that each of them applies to your situation. If you have not started building capital up yet, consider how you will be able to do that. If you have not been able to find a broker, consider that.

This book is full of ideas on how you can make sure that you are going to be the best options trader possible. Your portfolio will be filled with options trades that are good and profitable. You will also learn the basics that you need to know about hedges and even futures trading.

Are you ready to take your beginner knowledge to the next level?

INTRODUCTION

Congratulations on downloading your personal copy of *A Beginner's Guide to Options Trading*. Thank you for doing so.

The following chapters will discuss some of the many different aspects of options trading.

You will discover how important it is to make sure that you are getting a good deal on the trades that you do.

The final chapter will explore how options trading can work to give you passive income.

There are plenty of books on this subject on the market, thanks again for choosing this one! Every effort was made to ensure it is full of as much useful information as possible. Please enjoy!

CHAPTER 1: UNDERSTANDING TRADING AS A WHOLE

Trading is essentially the process of making money through smart decisions. You can buy and sell different pieces of companies and businesses, known as shares, through the process of trading. The beauty of this is that you are able to make money from it.

When you are trading, you will first start out by making an investment. This can be a large one or a small one, but most people start with just a small one so that they are not going to be out a lot of money if they happen to make a poor choice with the investment (as beginners often do). The point of trading is to have as little risk as possible when you are trading so that you will be able to keep things as profitable as possible, or break even at the very least.

After someone has initially invested in something, they will then allow it to sit for a period of time. Some people choose to just trade through the course of one day. They don't make a lot of profit at once, but they normally have many different investments that they are working with at any time. When they do this several days a week – known as day trading – the profits typically build up. Others, though, want to let their investments sit for a week, a month, a year, or sometimes even longer. When they do this, they watch the price of the investment closely and then when it is at its highest, they sell their shares for profit.

If you are planning to start trading at any point in your life, you need to know that there are differences in trading types and that you should stick to one type of trading. For example, if you have chosen options trading as your niche, you should not try to start real estate trading or investing in anything else other than what you started with.

Picking a niche is the only way that you will be able to turn into a professional. You need a niche so that you can focus on one thing. When you focus on only one thing, the experience that you gain is a lot more focused, a lot more valuable, and a lot more profitable. As a result, by working with niches, you also become a better investor.

Picking a niche like options trading is a great way to get started with trading and is something that most people will be able to handle when they are just getting started in their trading career. It is important to note that options trading isn't necessarily easy. In fact, it's not easy at all, and can be quite risky. However, it is something that you can learn in a short period of time.

If you are going to start options trading, you need to learn as much as possible about it so that you will be able to be successful at it; otherwise, you run the risk of making a poor investment and losing big. That's where this book comes in.

Chapter 2: Options Trading in a Historical Sense

Options trading is something that is currently very popular, and it is one of the biggest forms of financial trading in the world. Billions of dollars in contracts are traded on a yearly basis, and that is something that, obviously, has a huge effect on the economy in all areas of the world. Because of this, many believe that options trading in its current form has been around for hundreds of years, but that simply isn't true.

Options trading, as we know it today, started just about 50 years ago and has ballooned since then, becoming bigger and offering more trading opportunities for people who are thus interested. Because of the risky nature and historical tendency to lead to speculative bubbles, some investors are still leery about options trading.However, modern options trading is relatively safe.As an example of how young modern options trading is, the Chicago Board Options Exchange is one of the oldest modern options exchanges and it has only been around since the 1970s.

Looking at Futures vs. Options

Futures and options are really close to being the same thing. The biggest difference lies in the way that you are able to carry out the contract. For example, you are able to sell your options at any time that you want. With futures, you have to wait until the end of the contract if you want to be able to sell the investment and start to profit off of it.

Futures are very limiting while options are very flexible in terms of selling for a profit.

Ability to Sell Your Options

One of the biggest benefits to using options is that, as I said, you can sell them at any time that you want within a certain timeframe delineated in the contract. However, this also means that you need to make sure that you are going to truly profit from the options contracts that you have established.

Because there are so many different aspects that go into trading, especially when you have somethingso functional and important as options contracts, you will be able to look at the different key points of shares and contracts,as well as the way that they are building up value while you have them. Once you've evaluated everything, if you want to sell your options and the price is at a good point, you can stand to make a huge profit off of them.

Change in the Way That Options Work

Throughout time, people recognized that there was a need to have a way to speculate on future values. Many investors liked the way that trading worked and they especially liked the way that futures worked, but they did not want to have to wait until the end of the contract to be able to profit from the trades. This was something that they always kept in mind, but it took off when options trading became a reality. There are many ways that options trading works to help enterprising investors out, and allowing them the chance to sell their investments off at anytime that they want at a certain price point gives them the flexibility that many people hope for when they are trading and when they are doing different things.

Options in the Past

Despite the fact that options are a fairly new concept in the world of modern trading, the idea behind options trading is ancient. As far back as ancient times, people were speculating on certain markets. This was something that the modern traders to base their options trading ideologies on, and it allowed them the chance to make sure that they were truly doing things the right way by comparing their set-up to the mistakes of the past, such as the Dutch Tulip bubble.

Options trading historically served the same purpose it does today: a way for people to make money off of their intuition for judging market directions. While they did not necessarily call it options trading at the time and they certainly did not have the technology that is available today, the principles behind it were the same.

Having Regulations for Options

When futures trading first started, there were a lot of regulations for it, and people had to follow each of these regulations to make sure that they were going to be able to get the best experience possible when it came to the trading opportunities. In other words, the regulations served both the investors and the economy by preventing speculative bubbles.

The same is true for options trading. However, with options trading,the regulations didn't really start to pop up until after the *concept* of options trading had been long developed. Because of this, the process for developing regulations was a little different than it had been for futures, as the process for developing regulations for options trading had been based in the historical mistakes of speculative trading.

Obviously, having the ability to look at past options trading scenarios was helpful when the regulations were being made.

Looking to the past will invariably teach you a lot about the future. The same is true for options trading. There are a number of regulations in place based on the early mistakes of proto-modern options trading and early speculative markets.

In other words, the regulations for options trading may seem rather extensive, but they are as they are for very good reason.

CHAPTER 3: THE BASICS OF OPTIONS TRADING

There are a few things that you need to know before you start options trading. You need to know what options trading is, the basic language you will find in the trading world, why people choose to work with options contracts, the different orders that you can use with options trading, and the way that options work.

Definition of Options

Options are a type of trade that is in contract form. The buyer of the contract is then able to sell the asset that comes along with the contract at a specified time for a specified price. Essentially, it's a promise from one person to another to either buy or sell something at a given price, regardless of its real market price, at a certain point. The price does fluctuate both up and down when it comes to the total value of the options, as a response to the market price and the contract price. Because of this, you can be sure that you will almost always make a profit on the options if you know the right way to buy them and know the specific terms of the contract.

The biggest thing with options is that they do have an expiration date. If you do not have a chance to sell it off before that time, then you will lose your money because the contract is void.

Language You'll Hear in Options Trading

Call option – This is basically a contract in which Person A tells Person B that Person B is allowed to buy commodity/stock C at price x, regardless of market price y, as long as Person B exercises their contract by expiration date d.

Put option – The inverse of a call option; Person A tells Person B that Person B is allowed to *sell* commodity/stock C at price x regardless of market price y, as long as Person B exercises their contract by expiration date d.

Derivative – the total value of the security that comes from the purchase amount and the assets that stand underneath the total value of the contract

Expiration date – the point in which the contract will expire, and it will then not be able to make any more money. If a contract holder does not sell the contract before that time, he or she will lose out on the money that was paid for the contract.

Long position – The person who is buying an options contract is in the *long position*. They have the option, though not the obligation, to exercise the contract by a given date.

Options contract – the actual contract that is purchased as an investment. It outlines the price, the value that is going to come and the expiration date of the contract at which point it becomes completely useless to the people who have the contract and who want to be able to sell it.

Reasons for Options Trading

The two biggest reasons that most people use options trading as their main form of investment are speculation and hedging. When it comes to these two particular niches, options fill them out particularly well.

The speculation part is easy. Options trading allows you to essentially bet that stock/commodity c will rise to price y by date d. If you buy the stock/commodity c at price x, and it rises to price y – which just happens to be $10 more than price x – then you gain a total of $10 per share/unit in profit, if you turn around and sell the asset/commodity instantly at price *y*. You get the $10 in profit per share/unit because the options contract allowed you the ability to buy the stock/commodity *c* at price *x* even when the actual market price was *y*. So, with options trading, you can *assume* that an asset or commodity is going to rise in value massively for some reason or another, and then get an options contract *now* letting you buy it at a set price *later*, so that you can turn a profit simply selling the asset or commodity at market price.

Hedging, on the other hand, is one of the lowest risk tactics in options trading. The people who use hedging are able to get more out of the experiences that they have because hedging provides an assurance that their money will be safe. The options that you purchase will only be available so that you can reduce the amount of loss on your investments. If you are going to hedge with options, you need to make sure that you are doing it in combination with other stocks and trading options that you have.

How it All Works

If you have a contract that has different guarantees on it when it comes to finances, you will be able to use that contract to make sure that you are going to get more money from the various assets and commodities that you're working with. The market price of a stock that you have may be at a certain point at any one point in time. Then, the price may go up. Depending on what the options contract was written with, the price will go up with it. The contract is usually worth 100 times the rise in the stock because it is 100 shares worth of that fund.

For example, if you have an options contract that says you have 100 shares of a stock for company X, then when the price of the stock rises for company X, so does the value of your options contract. If company X goes from a value of $10 to $18, then your contract will also go up by eight points. Because you have 100 shares within that contract, it will actually be worth $800 more.

Orders for Options Trading

When you have an options contract, you will need to create some orders that will tell your broker to do specific things. These can be things like stopping the options from losing too much money or simply limiting the amount of money that gets spent on the options. If you know which order you want to use, you will be able to make sure that you are going to truly be able to have your broker do the best work possible.

Limit orders give your broker the price that you will buy or sell for.

Stop limit orders will limit the way that you are able to change your money around between different options trading contracts.

Market orders tell your broker to only act if the options stock is at a specific market price.

Stop market orders do the same as stop loss, but they are based on the market value of the options stock.

Stop loss orders are just like any other type of stop loss. You tell your broker where you want to stop losing money at.

CHAPTER 4: HOW TO GET STARTED WITH OPTIONS TRADING

One of the hardest parts of options trading is actually getting started with it. You will need to take several steps if you want to start trading and each of these steps will require you to do different things. The great part about stock options and options trading is that you will be able to use the previous starting points that you had with options trading if you ever make the decision to start a new type of trade. There are many different things that you can do when getting started out with stock options trading, and it's important that you give all of them ample thought.

Understand Your Goals

You should know what your objectives are before you start options trading. This is to help you have a clear idea of where you want to be when you are getting started, so that you can make sure that you are making all of the right options trading decisions for *you*. It can sometimes be difficult to know what you want to get out of stocks and trading.

Do you want to make a little money on the side? Do you want to replace your full-time income? Are you hoping for passive income?

Each of these things will help you to have a better understanding of the ultimate goal that you have in mind. You need to make sure that you are on the right path to get that which you want when you are looking at the different paths within an options trading career.

Try Strategies

There are several different strategies that will help you to have a better understanding of the way that options trading works. Following these strategies can be complicated at worst and stupidly simple at best. The majority of the strategies that people use for options trading are outlined in this book so that you can follow them and make sure that you are getting the best experience possible with trading.

Choose the one that best lines up with your capabilities and with the end goal that you have for your trading. If you know what you want to do with options trading and if you work to always make sure that you are getting to that point, it will be much easier for you to figure out the specific steps that you need to take while you are trading.

Always Use a Broker

Having a broker is one of the only ways to ensure that you will be able to be successful with options trading. A broker can not only help you get the best advice that you need for trades, but he or she will also help you to figure out where you need to go with each of the trades that you have. It is a good idea to try different things that the broker suggests and to make sure that you are going to be able to use these options when it comes time to trade. There are many different aspects of trading so be sure that you are paying attention to all of them.

The broker will not only be able to help you figure out what you need to do with trades and with the options contracts that you have but will also be able to help you figure out if you meet the requirements for being able to get involved in options trading.

Can You Participate?

There is a chance that you may not be eligible for options trading. About 30% of people who have the goal of options trading are not actually able to do the trades that they want to do. There are different factors that go into determining your eligibility, but the majority of them have to do with risk. If you are deemed to be high risk, if your portfolio is not large enough to satisfy the requirements, or if you show that you are somehow not able to fit options trading into your portfolio in a way that makes sense, you will not be able to participate in options trading.

Just like with other parts of trading, things can always change, though. Keep that in mind when you make the decision to try new things with options trading. You will be able to try new things, and you can even change your eligibility with time. Eligibility for options trading, indeed, is something that everyone can work toward.

Before you make the decision to invest in options trading, always check with your broker to make sure that you are eligible to do it.

The Trading Account

Once you have determined whether or not you are eligible for options trading, you will then be able to start your trading account. This is generally different from a traditional trade account in that it is a margin account. You can make sure that you are doing everything right with options contracts by starting up the margin account before you put the money into the stocks. It is a good idea to know what kind of account you are going to have and what the initial investment is going to look like for you when you start out with any sort of trading.

If you do not already have a margin account, you will need to talk to your broker about it. This is where all of the options trading actions will occur so you need to make sure that you are making a worthwhile decision about your trading account. This will essentially serve to make sure you're getting the most bang for your buck. You can also make sure that you are getting the best experience possible when your broker starts your margin account with you.

CHAPTER 5: THE DIFFERENT TYPES OF STOCK OPTIONS

There are different types of options contracts that you can choose from when you are getting started. The type of option contract that will work best for you will depend on the total capital that you have to put into the account along with the risk that you may carry. There are different things that you can choose from, and you should make sure that the options contracts that you act on line up with your goals.

Overview of Options

Options contracts largely depend upon the volatility of a stock and the amount of money which is invested. It is important to note that all of the different types of stock options can be deducted from that first initial capital function. It is a good idea to recognize that you will be able to put more money into the options stocks that you have within the contracts, but you will never have the option to lower your initial investment amount. You can always invest more but you can never uninvest without taking a potential loss.

Buying or Selling

When you are looking at the options contract that you have, it will be clear to see whether or not you are the buyer or seller. Your position will be outlined, and you will be able to figure out what the difference is between the two different parties. In each of the contracts that you have, you can only be the buyer or the seller.

For example, if you are the buyer of one contract, you will not have the opportunity to be the seller of that same contract. Instead, when you are ready to sell – and not just buy - options, you will need to make the decision to set up new contracts with assets that you already *own* (or intend to own). You can always ask your broker for assistance, here.

Striking Price

In the contract, the price is listed. The strike price is the point at which you can buy the option that is listed in the contract. It is important to note that you will not be able to buy before it reaches that price. Period.

If you are a buyer on the contract, you will also have a strike price at which you can sell. This tells you that you cannot sell until it hits the strike price. It is clear to see that this is much different from what is offered with futures. When there is a future, there is no specific strike price, but there is a strike date. The seller cannot sell before it reaches that point on the calendar. With options, you can still sell before it reaches any type of date (and you *should* sell before it hits the expiration, certainly) but you need to just be sure that it is at the right price.

The Expiration

Every single options contract will have an expiration date. This is something that must be closely monitored. For this reason, you are advised to have a broker. The broker will be able to tell you what you are doing and when the expiration date is approaching. If you find that you are getting close to the expiration date, you need to sell off the option even if your profit is not as high as what you would like it to be. If you don't, you'll lose the money that you initially put into the investment, and that can be a terrible way to start out with options trading.

Premium Investment

Your premium is basically the same as any other type of premium that you would see in investing and in stocks. It is the amount of money that you paid to purchase the options contract.

Make sure that your premium is enough to purchase the options contract but is not so much that you are going to lose a large amount of money on the trades that you are doing. You should always be careful with the stocks that you have,but options are a whole other ballpark of carefulness. Since they are somewhat of a risk, you definitely want to go for one that has a lower premium. If you do this, you will put yourself as a lower risk investment which will not only help you to lose less money but will also make you have a better appearance with your portfolio.

Style of Option

There are two main styles of options stocks.

American style – you can use the rights that you have in your contract at anytime that you have the contract in your possession. You do not have to wait until the actual expiration date so that you have more time to keep yourself from losing money. You can sell at any time after the price has hit the strike out amount.

European style – you are required to wait until the actual expiration date to be able to use that selling option. This can be a problem because it is sometimes difficult to sell a stock in one day. For example, you cannot sell the stock until you have reached the expiration date, but if you go for longer than the expiration date, you will lose out on the money that you have in your stock option contract. This is detrimental because you will not have that money that you put into the premium of the contract, so you will start out with a loss.

While the American option is the more popular among people who are trading, it is something that you will need to decide for yourself. Other than the expiration date specifics of each style, there are no major differences between the two styles of option contracts.

CHAPTER 6: CHOOSING INDEX OPTIONS

The Index Options are slightly different types of contracts, and working with them can drastically change the way that you are working with options contracts. They are simply another style that you can use when you are trading and when you have the different aspects of your trades lined up. When you choose to use an index option stock, you are simply choosing a different way that you can invest your money in the stocks that you think will be profitable.

Indexes

The most common type of index options that are available is the DJIA and the NASDAQ, which are both included in different sectors. The Dow Jones is included with companies that have very large caps on them. The initial investments, or premiums, are usually much higher with the DJIA. With the

NASDAQ, you will be getting an investment that is closer to the technological side of investing, but it will cost you much less money than if you were doing it in any other way.

Choices

You can choose any sector within the two major types of indexes. This will allow you the chance to make sure that you are going to be able to get the different benefits that come with the sectors. If you are particularly interested in a sector or if you find that it is one that seems to do well according to the research that you have done, you should make that choice. It can sometimes be difficult to decide what you have done and what you are going to do in the future. If you do not know what choice you are going to make, it is wise to check with your broker. While the broker will not be able to tell you which decision you should make, he or she can give you the various beneficial points that come with each of the investments.

Advantages

The best part about the index options is that you will be able to profit in several different sectors when it comes to investing. You can get your hands into the business of many different types of investments, and that will help you to get exactly what you need with your investing opportunities. You will also be able to make more money.

The more streams of income that you have that come from investing in general, the more you will be able to profit and the more you will be able to benefit from all of the different stock price increases.

If you are going to use index options for stocks, you should make sure that you are trying more than one sector. Doing this will enable you to truly get an understanding how each of the sectors works, as well as giving you the added perk of diversified investments.

Settlement

The cash that comes from index options is the settlement amount. Since you are not actually purchasing money or investing cash in the way that you would with traditional investments, you will need to make sure that you are converting your indexes into cash. While this can sometimes be difficult to do, you need to make sure that it is something that you are prepared for. The difference in the values of the index is calculated by using the strike price. What is leftover from the strike price is what you will collect on in cash. That is what your return will be.

Capping Index

The capped index options are available to people who have options contracts. They were created so that the index option can be sold off as soon as it reaches the cap. There is no other type of trading option that gives you this type of choice. When you are making the decision to invest in options stocks, you will need to determine whether or not you want to take advantage of the capped index options and whether or not that is going to be worth the extra amount that you need to do to get to that point.

Risk Leverage

When you are looking at the risks that are associated with Options contracts and the index style of these stocks, you will need to figure out which ones are the riskiest and which ones are going to bring a low risk to you. Of course, the lower that you put the premium, the lower the risk is going to be for the stock options so you should always keep that in mind when you are looking at stock options and at the different aspects that come with them. Be sure that you are always leveraging the risks that are associated with the trades so that you can make sure that you are putting all of the options that you have in your trading portfolio.

Multiplied Contracts

When you are choosing your index options, you can get a contract multiplier. This is something that will allow you the chance to cash out on the value of the index and of the options contract that is included with the index. Make sure that you are using the options contracts that you have to be able to get the best experience possible for your trade options. Always work to provide yourself with the best trades for your portfolio and for the different things that you are adding to it.

The Premium

As with traditional options stocks, you will need to pay the premium with cash. It's sad, but true; paying premiums is an absolutely necessary part of working with options. If you are using cash for your premium, you will then be able to get the multiplier and cash in on the amount that the options stock has built up for you over the period of time that you have had it in your portfolio.

Chapter 7: Choosing Currency Options

There are different trade options that will make a difference depending on the type of trade that you are doing. With options stocks, you can choose to use the index option, which is beneficial to people who do not want to deal in currency. The other option that is available, though, is currency. This is where you invest your money into the options stocks, and they are able to use the different types of currency within their own functions. This is something that is necessary if you want to be able to get the best experience possible and if you want to make sure that you are going to get your full investment back – and hopefully more.

While there are no multipliers with this type of options trade, there are different benefits that will help you to get back more cash when it comes to your trading. You do not have to worry about how much the trade value is going to change because the index does not play a part in this. You will simply have to worry about whether or not the currency that is present in these situations is fluctuating. If it is not, you can just collect on the amount that you initially put in as the financial premium.

The forex (Foreign Exchange) options provide a tool that traders and investors who are in the options contract trading business can use to make profit. They do not have to purchase the actual currency to be able to get to this point and simply have to use the leverage that they have within their portfolios so that they can make sure that they are getting the most out of the trading options available to them.

The contracts can be held when there is a currency options trade going on. This will help to reduce the amount of risk that occurs from trading and will help to prove that there will be profits from the different options that are included in all of the trades. When looking at trades, brokers and investors will both be able to see that a held contract is always a good way to reduce risk.

Choosing a currency option stock will always be lower risk than an index stock, but the payouts are often also much lower when you are using the currency trade models.

If you are using the forex model for your currency options trading portfolio, you will need to make sure that you are doing it the right way. There are different options when it comes to each of these, but they all involve the use of the forex system. If you do not want to use theforex, you will need to find a broker who does not participate in it. Brokers are not able to do forex options in addition to forex trading, because of the implications that come along with it. Investors, though, are actually able to choose two different brokers who do these things.

While there are regulations on the brokers and how they each can do the different things with the trading, there are very few on the investors when it comes to currency options trading. This is necessary for people who want to make sure that they are going to be able to get the most money possible from the trades that they are doing. It is also something that can help investors to realize what they are doing with the different trading options.

SPOT

The SPOT style of trading is intended for people who have a huge amount of startup capital they can use in order to get into forex trading. It is a high investment option and is generally not recommended for beginners, but some who have chosen it as their first options trading stock have done well with it. If you have the right broker who is able to use your stops and calls in the way that you want, you will be able to get a much better outcome from the SPOT trading option.

When you do Single Payment Options Trading, or SPOT, you will be able to bring about the different trading options. SPOT is created to automatically help you get the trades that you want. You can set up everything before you start trading and it will help you to get the payout options that you want. It will also give you the chance to be able to include all of the different aspects of trading. With SPOT, you will get a payment each time that you have made a prediction on the options trade and you are right. For those who are confident in their prediction skills, it can actually be worth the higher investment.

Call Options

The calling options that are included with the different forex styles operate almost identically to index options trading, but they are different in the sense that they involve real cash and currency that is going to change depending on the market and what is going on with the various businesses. If you know what you are doing, you will be able to call out the options and the information that is contained with each of them.

As you learn more about the call options and about the different things that are associated with the call options, you will be able to adjust the different types of options to your calling point. It is always a good idea to include the different things that are reduced with calling and putting the information into the algorithms. As you are learning more about the way that things are done in trading, the chances are that you will want to switch from this type of forex trade to one that allows you to get a single payment.

While call options are great for people who are just getting started in options trading, most usually move onto the SPOT model where they can get higher payouts for a slightly higher risk.

CHAPTER 8: ETF AND THE FUTURE OPTIONS

Just because options trading is slightly different from future trading does not necessarily mean that you can avoid everything about futures trading. It can sometimes be difficult to figure out exactly what you need to do to make sure that you are going to get each of the different options contracts to go your way; knowing more about everything related to options can help with this, including futures.

As you are looking at the options stocks, you should also consider the ETF, or exchange traded funds, along with the future options so that you can make sure that you are getting the best deal possible.

Exchange traded funds are the mutual funds of the options trading world. They are handled just like mutual funds, and they can be traded like stocks and shares are traditionally traded. If you are working with the different types of ETFs, you can look at them in the same way as mutual funds and trades.

You do not need to have a special margin account to be able to use ETFS. This is because they are available and it is legal to trade them on the regular stock exchange. You don't have to worry about the way that they are being traded or any of the implications that come along with using a smaller account or a margin account that could bring about problems in your portfolio. Always make sure that you are working with your ETFs in the same way that you would work with traditional stocks and shares.

Diversity

When you are using options trading, ETF is one of the best chances at gaining diversity in your portfolio. Since they can be traded on the open stock market, they are simple to add to your portfolio, and they can make a huge difference in the way that your portfolio looks. Always make sure that you are trying new things and that you are working to promote the different aspects of your portfolio. With ETF, you can see that there is a major difference in the way that stocks are traded in the field.

Larger Volumes

ETFs are also great if you want to have a large volume of stocks. They can be purchased in mass quantities, but the prices are generally close to the same of what a similar stock would cost you on the open market. Since they are slightly more complex than a traditional stock, they will eventually grow to be worth more than what the stocks are. This will give you the chance to see that they can be traded and they will be able to be purchased for different amounts. It is always a good idea to try out different stocks and to make sure that you have things like ETFs available in your trading portfolio so that you don't have to worry about the implications that come along with not having a diversified portfolio.

Risks

Perhaps one of the biggest benefits that come with ETFs is also their downfall. Since they are so complex, it is important to note that they cannot be used in the way that other stocks are able to be used. You must make sure that you are diversifying your portfolio heavily. Since you have them in there, you need to trade them.

If you have never had a complex stock like an ETF, you will want to check with your broker for advice on what can be done with the stock and the way that you can work to make sure that the stock is truly working for you.

Futures

Despite the fact that futures were the forerunner for options trading, they have not become completely obsolete just because options are now more prominent. In fact, there is actually a chance that futures have grown in popularity as a result of options trading. If you are hoping to diversify your portfolio even further, consider futures but also consider the implications that come with future trading options.

The Stock Exchange with Futures

Similar to options trading, you need to make sure that you have a specific margin account that was designed to be used with futures. This will help prevent you from running into major problems that could happen in the Open Stock Exchange. You cannot use futures on the stock exchange, and they will be separate from it despite the fact that the returns will be determined based on the stock exchange. Try to find the best margin fund for your futures so that you can have them separate from your options trading.

Pricing

The premium that you would typically see with a future is usually about the same as what you would see with options stocks. This is because they are very similar. Where you must wait for the date with futures, you must wait for the price with options stocks. It is a good idea to always try and make sure that you are dividing your investments evenly between the two so that, if you lose out on one, you will still have a chance to profit on the other.

Strike Dates

There is no expiration date on the futures. This is because they are meant to go infinitely unlike the options trading. There is, however, a price that you must reach before you can buy or sell the contract. That is the downside to the trades and is something that propelled the reasoning behind the options trading. It is important to know that you cannot sell unless you are at that price. You must also be able to reach a future date before you can sell. Without the expiration date, you don't have to be in such a hurry to sell, but you *do* have to wait a specified amount of time.

CHAPTER 9: OPTIONS TRADING STRATEGY

TERMS

You should never jump into options trading without knowing the implications of it and the various things that you can do to make the trades better. You need to know the strategies that are available to traders, if you want to ever have a chance at making things work out within your trade portfolio. It can be easy to get caught up in the problems that come along with options trading, so make sure that you are always following the prescribed strategies so that you do not miss out on the money that you *could* be making from each of the trades.

To get the best advice on the strategies, you will need to know the terms that are used.

Bull – investor who wants to make the market asset increase. It is someone who buys up the assets and then sells them once it increases. Functions as a traditional type of investor.

Bull spread – when the bulls work to make sure that they are able to get the different things that they want in the options trading. They will often buy up several different trade options, and then they will sell them quickly. They operate as professionals and are often able to predict when there is going to be a change in the market.

Bear – completely opposite from bulls. They look for decreases in the market, and they sell off their options trades in anticipation of the drop in the price. They will then repurchase them at the lower price later on when the prices do go down.

Bear spread – the same thing as a bull spread but opposite on the level that they sell and re-buy the trades that they have worked with before.

Downside – when the hedging tool helps you to limit the loss that you have on your assets. It is often used in combination with options contracts so that you can make sure that you are getting the most out of the other types of investments that you have in your own portfolio.

Vertical – the investor wants to sell and buy at the same time. This usually does not happen exactly at the same time, but it is within a few seconds of the happening that comes along with the trades. It is necessary for investors to make sure that they are losing out on the bad deals and gaining profits on the good options trades.

Collar – another type of protection that will work similarly to hedging and will provide the investor with the security that they need when there is a huge dip in the stock market. By putting a money option into the options trade and then writing the option as if he or she were out of money, they can make sure that they are using the collar to protect themselves.

Straddle – when an investor is riding both of the options that they have. They can actually do this with more than one option, but it is usually difficult to do so especially for investors who are just starting out. They must then make a decision which one they are going to jump on and take the investment opportunity with.

Strangle – the way the investor is able to work with two completely different types of investments. The investor will do all of these different things at the same time, and the intent is for the option contracts to increase in value. Investors should know which direction each of the options are going and they should be confident in the fact that they are doing different things. If an investor does not know the direction that the investment is going in, there are implications that can often cause the investor to lose the money that they have put into the options trades.

Butterfly trading – this is similar to a vertical trade, but it is different in that itis on a much larger scale. It involves using several different options trades and making sure that they are being simultaneously sold and purchased at the same time. An investor will do this if he or she thinks that there is going to be a big change in the market. By selling and buying at the same time, he will set himself up for the changes that are going to come in the market, and it will make things much easier when the change *does* happen to the market – whether it is a drop or a rise in the price.

If you are able to look at each of these terms and know what they mean in a grander sense, you are then ready to move onto the next chapter. If you feel that you are still not familiar with them, study them and apply them to real world situations.

The easiest way to practice the terms, learn what they mean, who they apply to, and the way that you can use them on your own is to create a practice scenario. Figure out the trading scenario that you want to come up with and label each of the parts of it. If you are confident with your trading terms, you should then try to learn the different aspects of the trades and what they will mean to you.

It is always a good idea to make sure that you are familiar with the basic terminology because that is just the starting point.

While these terms are helpful and they can create a better outlook for you while you are investing, you will be able to learn much more when you start the true trading process. You will quickly find that these are just a starting point and that there are so many more points that you will need to keep track of when you are doing different things in the trading field. Always learn as much as you can and make note of it. Consider keeping these terms handy so that you can use them later on.

CHAPTER 10: THE OPTIONS TRADING STRATEGY

Learning the different types of strategies that are available to you will help you to make the right choice when it comes time for you to start trading and getting the profits that you desire from the trades that you make. It is a good idea to be sure that you know which strategy is going to work for you based on the goals that you have set up for yourself. When you are working to make sure that you are choosing the right type of strategy, you can figure out which options line up with the goals that you have and how you want to involve all of the different aspects.

Long Position

People who want to buy a lot before the price increases generally use this type of strategy. If you want to create a large profit over a long period of time, you can take advantage of having a long position available to you.

Since you can base your position off of the leverage that you are going to get from the trading options, you will be able to use the leverage to your advantage. If you have a very strong portfolio, the long position will work the best with you.

If you are going to invest your money, consider doing so with the $5,000 model in the shares that you are going to use. If the average price of the shares is $127, you can get 39 shares out of the company. If you want to add just a bit more money, you can get the full 40 shares out of the company. If the shares go up over the period of time that you have them in, your shares' value will go up, too. When you are investing in the shares, you need to keep in mind that it sometimes takes a long time to get a return on the shares. In the short time that the shares went up by just a few dollars, you would have profited only around $120. If you wait just a little longer, the shares will probably rise again, and you will be able to profit even more from the initial investment that you made. The long position takes patience and time, but it is often worth it if you want to get the highest profits possible.

Short Position

You can purchase the stocks for a short position if you do not want to risk a lot of money. Wait until the price goes way down before you buy them and then allow yourself the chance to purchase them at a low price. Before they drop again, sell them. This would make you a bearish type of trader in a market that is bullish. You can try different things with short positioning, but you will almost always profit more if you can sellthe shares for a profit quicker. After you have sold them (before the decrease), you should wait until the decrease happens. When it does, use the profit that you received from selling them and then buy them back up again. Do this over and over again until the market stops decreasing.

Most of the people who are taking options trading approaches for the first time will generally use this type of strategy. It is safer than long positioning, it brings profits in right away, and it makes it easier for people to be sure that they are going to get the best return possible for the trades that they have. It is also something that will show you how much money you *can* make from options trading so that it will give you a boost at the beginning.

Calling Covers

If you combine the short and the long positions together, you will get the strategy that most people use once they are comfortable with both short and long. You should first learn the short position. Next, take a bull approach and try to use the long position. From there, you can combine them both. Buy stocks when they are very low and hang onto them until they are very high. Sell them off before the decrease and then repurchase them so that you can make sure that you are making money when they are at the lowest amount possible. If you want to be able to get the best experience possible with your trading, you will be able to learn both short and long positioning.

There is not a single investor out there who is successful and who only uses either short or long positioning. All of the best investors will be able to use both of them in combination with each other so that they can make sure that they are getting the best experience possible. It is necessary for investors to make sure that they are going to be able to do everything that they can when it comes to their position.

Protection

There are times when you may come across options trades that seem like they are going to be risky. You may see that their returns are going to be great but the initial investment is very risky and something that you will have to weigh against the potential benefits. If you go for this risky sort of investment, consider the protection that comes with it.

Similar to how you use options stocks to create a hedge for your traditional trading, you can also use hedges for the options stocks. This will help you to make sure that you are protected and that you are going to be able to be as protected as possible from any negative ramifications. You can be unafraid to take risks that are associated with trading when you know that you have a hedge in place that can protect you. Be sure that you do this when you know that the rewards are going to be better than what some of the risks are. Your financial protective structures will help to balance the weight with the problems.

CHAPTER 11: ENSURING SUCCESS WITH OPTIONS TRADING

There is no way to guarantee that you are going to be successful 100% of the time with any type of trading, especially options trading. The idea behind options trading is that it is slightly riskier than any other type of trading, but on the other hand, if you do it the right way, you will witness some of the largest returns you will ever see across any form of trading. The general idea in the world of finance is that the amount of risk is correlative to the amount of reward. This is true even with options trading. It may be hard to figure out the right way to do it but following each of these tips will guarantee that you have given yourself a chance to make money from the trades that you have initiated.

Build Capital

Before you start investing in any way, you need to build up capital. You cannot expect to have good returns on an investment if it is just a small amount. While you may be very proud of yourself for having 100 dollars in your bank account, the bad news is that this is just not enough to get started with investing. If you want to be able to even come close to purchasing worthwhile options contracts, you will need far above $1,000 to get started. You can get cheaper ones… but the thing is that those contracts are cheap for a reason.

Keep saving, and you will, eventually, have the money that you need to invest. By the way, are you using a high-interest savings account to save that money? You should be!

Wise Investment

No matter what type of options trade you are going to get involved in, you need to make sure that the investment is one that makes sense. Do all of the required research on the company before you invest your money into it. If you don't do this, you will risk not getting the return that you want from the investment. An investment is an *investment*. Why would you invest into something that you know nothing about? You will probably struggle at first when it comes to all of the different aspects of options trading, and you may find starting out that it's even a bit overwhelming. However, always try your best and keep a close eye on the different market approaches to trading. Wisdom comes solely from experience.

Take (Some) Risks

There are always going to be risks with trading. Whether they are risks dealing directly with your capital supply or risks dealing more specifically with your different investitures is dependent upon how good of a trader you are. Be sure that you work hard to take the right kind of risks and that you are taking the right kind of chances. You should learn what you are comfortable with when it comes to the risks that you are going to take. How much do the benefits outweigh the risk? Is the benefit big enough that it will be worth it if you lose the money that you put into the investment? If your answer is no, you probably should not take the risk.

Adjust Your Positioning

If you find that you are struggling to get the positioning right with your investment, you should change it. This does not mean that you will make a huge switch from a long position to a short position or the other way around, but it does mean that you will need to make sure that you are going to get the best return possible from wherever you are. Take specific and special pains to write down how you are performing from both the short and long positions. Consider the results. Do you consistently perform badly in the long position? Look at what's happening in those trades – every aspect – and see where things are going wrong. In the end, if you are finding that your position isn't working, just try your best to change it and to make sure that you will be able to include different options with the positions that you initially set out to take.

Re-Invest the Money

When you make money, you need to reinvest that money. With the money just sitting there, you are not going to be able to earn more on it. Since you have the money in the first place, take the smallest amount of profit off of it to pay yourself and then reinvest the rest of the money so that you can, quite simply, use your profits in order to turn more profits.

Broker Experience

When you are shopping for a broker, make sure that the broker who you are going to work with has experience in options trading. There may be brokers who have years of experience on the open stock exchange, but they may not have any idea about the options trading sector. This can mean different things for different people, but it is always a good idea to make sure that you get pertinent and up-to-date information from your broker. If your broker *does* have experience with options trading, make sure that it is the kind of experience that you are looking for and that it is something that you can use to make your trading options more professional. This is especially important if you have never traded before and if you want to get the best trading profits possible. Does your broker have a positive history with the options trading sector? Do what you can to find out.

Don't Put All Your Eggs In One Basket

Make sure that you are trying different types of options trades. If you have a lot of money to invest, don't invest it all in one type of options trading. Instead, invest it in several different options contracts that seem like they would be a good fit for your portfolio. Always do your best to ensure that you are choosing *good* options contracts and that the trades that you have are ones that will make the most sense for you and your portfolio.

Consider the Payout

You need to keep the end game in mind each time that you try to invest in different things. The end game, of course, is the payout that you are going to be able to get when you exercise an options contract. If you are looking for different options that are within your trading budget, you will need to make sure that you are doing everything that you can to include these new potential option contracts.

Try Something New

Trying new things is a great way to ensure that you are going to be able to get the highest profit possible. If you are not aware of the different profits that come from different trade options, you – quite simply – are just going to remain inexperienced and won't ever become a masterful options trader. Each time that you decide to invest again, take a look around. Take into account all of the information available to you about every single stock on the various markets that you're looking at.

CHAPTER 12: IS PASSIVE INCOME POSSIBLE WITH OPTIONS TRADING?

Many people look for passive income. They put a lot of work into their trading in the beginning so that they do not have to do as much later on and so that they can make sure that they are going to continue profiting for years to come. What most people don't know, though, is that it is actually difficult to gain passive income from things like options investing.

Set It Up

You can prepare for passive income by always setting up your options trading with the things that you want it to do. You should have a good idea of the way that it works and the different things that you can do with options trading before you try to step back and away from the different things that happen in trading. You can expect to be options trading for at least five years before you know the different things that will set you up for passive income success. When you have done this, and you are constantly recycling the money that you have made back into the investments, you will know that you are ready to try to make passive income.

You Need a Broker

While you should have a broker who is helping you with your options trading already, you will need a broker who will be able to help you run the whole operation. This can be the regular broker that you have been using the whole time or it can be someone new who specializes in the type of passive income that you want to be able to make. If you find a good broker who is also able to help you with your passive income goals, you should rely on that one to do it for you when you try to make passive income.

Automation

There are certain things that you can use in order to automate the trading process. This will not work all of the time if you are doing options trading, but you can make sure that you have certain safeguards in place that will allow you to make passive income. The whole process cannot be completely automated – that's what your broker is for – but automation *is* something that will take a lot of the pressure off of the whole affair of options trading. Computers are, in some ways, smarter than people. They can be programmed to make the best decisions and every computer error is simply a human error coming back down the line.

Use Stops

Stop losses, limits, and protocols can all be put in place to ensure that you don't lose *too* much money. This means that you will need to figure out the right way to do each of these things and that you will need to include all of these different things with your assets and options trading. Always make sure that your broker knows where you want to stop the loss or limit the trades at so that you don't lose all of the money that you have built up in the time leading up to when you started to take a more hands-off approach to the deals.

In closing, yes, you can make passive income with options trading. It is not easy, though, so you may want to just keep doing options trading on your own and profiting off of it in that way. If you'd like to make passive income off of it though, it is most certainly possible. You need a very good and competent broker behind you, too.

CONCLUSION

Thank for making it through to the end of *A Beginner's Guide to Options Trading*. Let's hope it was informative and able to provide you with all of the tools you need to achieve your goals of making money through the various options trading sectors.

The next step is to start saving up your money or to head out on your search for the perfect broker who will help you learn as much as you can about the trades that will one day make you rich.

Finally, if you found this book useful in any way, a review on Amazon is always appreciated!

Options Trading: The Ultimate Guide to Options Trading Uncovering Options Trading Profit Making Secrets

Description

If you have ever spent any real time trading in one or more of the asset investment markets, then you know how little freedom you sometimes have to go your own way and set your parameters for financial success as they make sense to you. Not so with options trading, which, as the name implies provides you with the option, not the obligation to carry through on what you have started. What's more based on the state of the market at the moment, you can easily transfer all of your existing skill into this new way of trading without missing a beat. If you are already somewhat familiar with options trading but want to take your skills to the next level then *Options Trading: The Ultimate Guide to Options Trading* is the book you have been waiting for.

Studies show that barely more than 10 percent of all options traders display the type of mindset that will help them be successful in the long term. Inside you will learn not just what it takes to form the type of mindset that will lead you to success, you will also learn important tips that the best options traders utilize on a daily basis along with the mistakes that many traders of all skill levels fall into and how you can avoid them for yourself. You will also learn what a reliable options trading plan looks like and how to measure the metrics of your current system to ensure that it measures up.

When it comes to being successful in the options trading market, it is all about the strategies that you use which is why inside you will find more than a dozen different strategies that are proven effective. You will find strategies that you will use every day as well as those which are going to be useful in more specialized situations. No matter your skill level or experience, *Options Trading: The Ultimate Guide to Options Trading* has something you can use.

If you know that you have it in you to be successful in the asset market, but you haven't quite found the right niche, then what are you waiting for? Take control of your financial future and buy this book today!

Inside you will find

- The difference between liquid and illiquid options and which you stay away from more often than not.

- Why it is important to consider historical volatility before you make any moves.

- Which metrics you are going to want to consider in order to determine if your trading plan is a dud or a financial stud.

- Ten different trading strategies for all seasons and market moods and how to get the most out of each one.

- Several specialized and advanced trading techniques and when to use them for maximum profit.

- *And more...*

INTRODUCTION

Congratulations on downloading *Options Trading: The Ultimate Guide to Options Trading* and thank you for doing so. When it comes to jumping into investment trading, options are easier than many other choices only because they rely more on existing knowledge of the underlying asset markets. This doesn't mean it is a straightforward process, however, and if you aren't careful, you can lose the sum total of your trading capital just as quickly as anywhere else.

To help ensure you are as successful as possible, the following chapters will discuss everything you need to know in order to ensure your time spent trading options is as easy and fruitful as possible. First, you will learn all about the mindset you need to adopt if you are going to be successful at options trading, not just in the short term but for the long term as well. From there you will learn many of the essential tips for success that experienced options traders use every day as well as the mistakes that many traders of all skill levels fall into and how you can avoid them for yourself. You will also learn about the importance of analyzing your trades and how to make sure that your trading system or plan is as efficient as possible. Finally, you will learn all about the many different trading strategies that you will use on a regular basis as well as several more specific trading strategies that can lead to major profits if utilized successfully. When you are finished there will be no option, no matter how convoluted that can stand in your way.

There are plenty of books on this subject on the market, thanks again for choosing this one! Every effort was made to ensure it is full of as much useful information as possible, please enjoy!

CHAPTER 1: THE MINDSET OF THE SUCCESSFUL OPTIONS TRADER

Studies show that barely more than 10 percent of all options traders display the type of mindset that will help them be successful in the long term. If you ever hope to be one of them, the first thing you need to do is to separate your emotions from your actions. Instead of letting your emotions factor into your trading strategy you need to remove them from the equation entirely by striving for the purely logical mindset that the best options traders cultivate. Following the suggestions outlined below will allow you to focus on long-term success regardless of what distractions are currently taking place around you, naturally improve your successful trade ratio in the process.

Have the right expectations: When it comes to honing your trader's mindset, perhaps the most important thing you can do is understand the results you are likely to experience. Having realistic expectations will allow you to respond appropriately both in times of failure as well as success. Specifically, this means you are going to want to banish thoughts of major success in a short period of time. This, in turn, will make it easier for you to prevent negative thoughts from creeping in throughout the day and causing you to take risks you otherwise would not take.

Additionally, it is important to be aware of what your emotional triggers are while trading. As everyone's triggers are different, the best way to understand your own is to keep a trading journal. In this journal, you are going to want to keep track of all of your trades, both successful and unsuccessful. You are going to want to note the date of each trade, the specifics surrounding it, the emotions you felt at the time, whether or not it was successful and why.

This exercise will not only help you to be aware of the emotions you are likely to experience in the future; it will help you understand why they appear in the first place. Emotions are the enemy of good trades and the best way to outpace your enemy is to know them inside and out.

For many traders, the strongest emotional triggers occur because they believe that correctly executing on a plan should lead to success 100 percent of the time. This stems from a misunderstanding of what considering a plan successful actually means. When it comes to options trading, a successful plan is one that hovers around a 60 percent success rate. This means that the scheme is extremely likely to turn a profit in the long run but a full 40 percent of the time it is used it will end in failure.

Losses are an unavoidable part of the investment process as risk is what ultimately leads to profit. If every investment were a guaranteed success, no one would bet against it, and there would be no chance for a profit. To mitigate these feelings, it is important to understand that a good trade is not one that made money but rather one that followed your system to the letter. In order to do so properly, you need to focus exclusively on your long-term results and treat everything else as meaningless noise.

This means you will want to wait at least a month between periods where you update your plan as anything less isn't going to provide you with enough details to make changes effectively. A significant moment in your evolution as an options trader will be the moment you can see why the trader who struck it rich after a few random trades is less successful than a trader with a few different plans that are always executed on properly no matter what. Remember, an effective trader is a selective trader.

Additionally, it is important to view options trading as a marathon rather than a sprint. With this fact in mind, it will be much easier for you to consider unsuccessful trades as a learning experience rather than an abject failure. This will then make it easier to keep emotions out of the equation, a feat that will become even easier with practice.

Understand that sometimes it is okay to do nothing: Another negative mindset that many traders foster hinges on the idea that they always need to be trading. The reality is that inaction can be just as profitable as an extended trading day if the conditions are right. As long as you are not the writer of an option then creating a pull or call doesn't force you to take any specific action if things don't work out in your favor. This fact may seem obvious, but when thought about logically, it becomes difficult to put theory into practice when there is money on the line.

This is why it is important to include situations where not going through with a trade is the right choice in the system that you decide to use. Once again, as long as you listen to the system that you created when your mindset was at its best you have the potential to become an expert options trader.

One of the most important things you need to wean out of your trading habits is jumping into trades without thinking them through entirely. Getting into the habit of picking and choosing the best trades for your system will help you become a professional when it comes to separating the wheat from the chaff. Knowing how to do this will contribute to ensuring that you are not just getting lucky now and then when it comes to making trades.

The same goes for getting out of a trade that turned sour as sticking with it and hoping things turn around is on of the easiest ways to lose your shirt. The best choice is always going to be letting the trade in question speak for itself and, if the trade doesn't go the way you expect, use that as an opportunity to learn for next time.

Put more value on patience: Patience is one of the most important, and most difficult, thing for many traders to learn. This is because sitting idly by with money on the table is such a difficult skill to master. Luckily, like all skills, it can be improved with practice. In order to perfect this skill, it is important to internalize the fact that the market isn't always making big moves, even at times of peak volatility. A useful way of helping yourself learn patience is by never focusing on just one trade at a time. Keeping your options open makes it easier to put each trade in perspective and prevent any one trade from artificially inflating its importance in your mind.

This is not to say that individual trades should be treated flippantly. Rather, you need to consider each trade in a perspective that takes the entirety of your goal into account. Additionally, this means that you are going to want to come to terms with the fact that there will be some days where there just isn't much going on. Overtrading can be just as damaging to your bottom line as not trading enough or making bad trades, especially if your transaction fees are higher than you might prefer.

To help cultivate the right mindset you are going to want to set either monthly or weekly profit goals as opposed to daily trading goals. Setting daily goals will likely cause you to make erratic trades at the end of the day as you strive to meet your goal. Even if you do end up making the target amount each day to hit your goal, it is likely that at least some of these trades will not have stood up to the strict level of scrutiny that a good plan requires. What's worse, if you end up seeing results based on the poorly thought out trades then it can promote the formation of destructive habits moving forward.

It is important to focus on building the type of discipline that will serve you well in the long term as early in your trading career as possible as you will less be less likely to have major trades on the line. The longer you go without giving into your impulses, the easier it will be to ignore them completely.

Learn to adapt: While it is important to stick to your system when your emotions are telling you otherwise, it is equally important to understand that sometimes market situations will change on the fly. When this occurs, you are going to need to go off the book if you hope to see your current trade end in profit. At first, it is going to be difficult to determine when it is the right time to toe the line and when it is the right time to experiment as the only clear indicator is practice.

In order to ensure that you have to fly blind as infrequently as possible, you are going to want to have several different trading plans on hand that is ideal for different market states. Learning which plan is right for which situation and when it is time for a change, in real time, will help you see much greater overall returns a much greater portion of the time.

Regardless of your planning, sometimes the unexpected will occur which means that you will need to make a leap of faith in order to be successful. A competent trader will be aware of market signs that change is on the horizon and will be able to act accordingly. This is another skill that cannot be taught; it can only be gained by experience.

As long as you keep the appropriate mindset regarding individual trades, any new strategy that is attempted will result in valuable data, if nothing else. It is important to understand that learning not to use a specific course of action a second time is always valuable, no matter the costs. Working to build this into your core trading mindset will lead you to greater success in a wider variety of situations in the long term.

Put consistency above all else: When it comes to developing a professional trading mindset, you are going to need to learn to prioritize consistency in all things. This can be another fact that is easy to understand in theory but much more difficult to put into practice. In order to get to this point, you will need to deal with financial setbacks and profits that were less than they first appeared. Ensuring these types of situations don't happen in the future requires a level of inquisitiveness that isn't innate for many traders. Making a habit of digging deeper into the reasons behind your successes as well as your failures is sure to lead to a greater level of success overall.

While certain types of investment market trading lend themselves to high risk/high reward strategies, trading options is not one of them. The best options traders tend to prioritize reliable gains of middling size and leave the riskier trades to the novices. While a larger than average return is nothing to sneeze at, a reliable trading record is going to generate a greater level of gain in the long term.

Understand your strengths and weaknesses: In order to find success in the long term, it is important that you understand where your trading strengths and weaknesses lie. Only by reaching this level of personal understanding will you ever be able to create a trading plan that builds on the one while minimizing the other. This is another reason it is so important to keep a trading journal as it will help to reveal tendencies that you tend to repeat that you might not otherwise be aware of.

Doing so will help you to become more aware of when you are letting emotions cloud your judgment as it will be clear when you made trades that you would not have made at the beginning of the day when your head was clear. With enough practice, you will then be able to head these emotions off at the pass and take a break instead of letting your successful trade percentage suffer.

Focus on keeping a clear mind, and you will find that not only is it easier to stick to your system but that you are able to determine the specific causes for success or failure found in each trade as well. Practice keeping this mindset during every trade, and you will see a greater percentage of successful trades sooner than you may expect.

CHAPTER 2: TIPS FOR SUCCESS

Avoid call options that are out of the money: While most investment markets focus on the trend of buying low and selling high, this approach doesn't work when it comes to options trading. Putting your money on out of the money call options often devolves into little more than gambling, and there are more effective ways of gambling that have much higher odds of success. Additionally, making these types of trades can make it difficult for you to understand why the trade failed to return a profit which makes the whole thing an exercise in futility.

To understand why out of the money call options are a poor choice it is important to keep in mind that when you purchase an option, you are saying not only that you know how the underlying asset is going to move but also when that move is going to occur. If you make a mistake when judging either, you are going to be out the premium you paid for the option along with the cost of the commission as well. What's worse, your funds will then be tied up until the option expires meaning you may miss out on a preferable alternative in the interim. Remember, in order to see a return on this type of trade the underlying asset of an option that is out of the money needs not only to increase, it also needs to reach all the way to the strike price.

Know when to use varying strategies: Options trading offers up a wide variety of different strategies to ensure you don't end up trying to fit square pegs into round holes. For example, buying on spread will sometimes be an excellent way to capitalize on various market conditions, but only if you are aware of the specifics beforehand. Not only will focusing on a single strategy cost you money in the long run, but it will also skew your results by calculating false losses that were not indicative of the strength of the system in question.

Know the spread: A long spread is made up of a pair of options that are similar in every way except one has a higher strike price than the other. The option with the higher cost is being purchased while the other is being sold. These options can be either puts or calls. Long spreads comprised of calls are bullish, and those comprised of puts are bearish.

Despite the fact that when the time lapse hurts one-half of the spread, it helps the other, spreads ultimately hurt your profit potential in most cases. This is because one-half of the pair is practically always going to expire unless the underlying asset is extremely volatile. With that being said, if you are interested in reliability above all else then they are still a good choice.

Always have a clear point of entry and exit: To trade in the options market successfully, it is important to always have a clear idea of the ideal entry and exit points you are going to utilize.

Not only will doing so help to mitigate the influence that emotion might have on each trade, but it will also ensure that you remain in the black over the long term. While it can be difficult to exit a trade when there is still the potential of money on the table, it is important to keep in mind that the potential for loss is also ever present. Setting a reasonable exit point and sticking with it is going to generate a larger profit over a prolonged period of time, guaranteed.

Avoid doubling up: If you are in the middle of a trade that appears to be going well and it suddenly turns around apparently at random, it is only natural to want to do anything you can to save it. Unfortunately, the best option virtually every single time is going to be to cut your losses and move on. In this situation, it is important to keep in mind that options are derivatives which mean the price is likely to change, and 'doubling down' is likely only going to lead to a greater overall loss.

While doubling down might feel like the right move at the moment, if you take the time to consider the amount of related time decay you are dealing with it can help to clear your head. If you still can determine what the right course of action is going to be all you need to do is to take an extra moment to clear your head and consider what you would have done in this situation if you weren't already committed. Nine times out of 10 the correct decision is going to be just to cut your losses and move on.

Stay away from illiquid options: Illiquidity measures the speed at which a specific option can be either bought or sold without causing the price to shift noticeably. Liquidity, on the other hand, can be thought of as the chance that the second trade of a given underlying asset will take place at the same price as the first. The stock market tends to be more liquid than the options market simply because there are fewer options related to each individual stock. As a result, you are automatically 10 percent more likely to end up on the losing side of a trade if you choose to move forward with an illiquid option.

Be willing to buy back short options: While, in theory, it might seem like buying back short options at the last moment is the best choice, this practice is sure to hurt you more than help you in the long run. It may be tempting to hold onto profitable options in order to squeeze the maximum return out of each investment, but you need to be aware that the potential for a reversal is always lurking in the shadows. Instead, a good rule of thumb is to buy back options that are currently at 80 percent of your ideal return or higher and let the extra take care of itself. While it may hurt to leave some potential profit on the table, it will improve your overall reliability, netting you a profit in the long run.

Keep earnings and dividend dates in mind: It is important to keep an eye on any underlying assets that you are currently working with as those who are currently holding calls have the potential to be assigned early dividends, with greater dividends having an increased chance of this occurrence. As owning an option doesn't mean owning the underlying asset, if this happens to you, then you won't be able to collect on your hard-earned money. The Early assignment is largely a random occurrence which means that if you don't keep your ear to the ground, it can be easy to get caught unaware and be unable to exercise the option before you miss the boat.

Along similar lines, you also want to be aware of when the earning season is going to take place for any of your underlying assets as it is likely going to increase the price of all of the contracts related to the underlying asset in question. Additionally, you will need to be caught up on current events as even the threat of influential news can be enough to cause a significant spike in volatility and premiums as well. In order to minimize the additional costs associated with trading during these periods, you are going to want to utilize a spread. Doing so will minimize the effect that inflation has on your bottom line.

Respond to an early assignment in the right way: When it comes time to sell the options you have purchased it is important to keep the possibility of early assignment in mind. To avoid unpleasantness, you are going to want to avoid lower-striking the long option in order to generate enough of the required underlying asset. Rather, you are going to want to place the long option onto the open market which will provide you with the chance to profit from the premium caused by the remaining time. You can then use your new funds to purchase the underlying asset that you are on the hook for, netting a profit in the process.

When you come up against an early assignment, it is important not to let your emotions get the better of you. Remember, the early assignment is more or less random so there is little you can do to prevent it from happening. Other traders aren't always going to make the best choices, and all you do is to roll with the punches. All you can do is to try and negate the chances of it affecting you as much as possible by being prepared for it depending on the mood of the market and its current level of volatility.

If you are going to utilize a spread, do it all at once: While purchasing a spread in a two-step process might seem like a good way to maximize profit, in reality, you are playing with fire. Specifically, purchasing a put or a call and then waiting to purchase the other half of the spread often leaves you open for the possibility of a reversal that will cost you more than what you would have made had things gone your way. Purchasing a spread as a single unit minimizes the number of variables that you have to contend with and increases your chance of success in the long term.

Take advantage of index options: Index options are a safe choice when the market is currently sporting a high degree of vulnerability. Index options are much less likely to experience sudden changes to a majority of news reports unless the results are extremely far reaching. The larger the index, the more likely it is that it will remain neutral.

On the other hand, if the market is in a holding pattern then you are going to want to consider short spreads on indices. In order to do so, you are going to want to choose an option pair with different strike prices in the standard fashion. This will largely remove time decay from the equation while also guaranteeing that you will make a profit as long as prices don't decrease.

Avoid making trades you cannot afford to lose: Regardless of how airtight your trading system appears to be, it is important to make it a habit of never investing more than you can afford to lose. No single trade is ever going to offer up enough of an incentive that taking the risk of knocking yourself out of the trading game entirely makes sense. Ensure that you know your limits beforehand for the absolute best results. In fact, a good rule of thumb is to never commit more than 2 percent of your total trading capital to any one trade. If you take this into account, then you would have to make 50 bad decisions in a row to lose all of your capital. If this occurs, you are likely focusing on the wrong investing and should consider your options carefully before continuing.

CHAPTER 3: MISTAKES TO AVOID

Not paying attention to the difference between implied volatility and historical volatility: When looking to trade successfully, implied volatility should be one of the primary ways to determine if a given option is priced correctly. Generally, the greater the amount of implied volatility, the more bearish the market will become and the more expensive most options sell for. However, historical volatility is just as important when it comes to choosing profitable options.

Historical volatility should also be determined beforehand so you can decide if the difference warrants further study. If this turns out to be the case, then you are going to want to take the time to go back at least 12 months with the underlying asset in the question in order to get a good baseline for the current state of things. While this can be time-consuming, it will ultimately be worthwhile if you find out things are not as they initially seemed.

Don't ignore probability: It is important to keep in mind that the historical data that you have access to will not apply to the current trend that the market is experiencing at all times. This means that to be successful, you are going to want to consider the probability as well as the odds that the market is going to behave expectedly. The probability is the ratio of the likelihood of a given outcome. Taking the time to understand the probability of a given outcome can make it easy to purchase the right options at the right time in order to minimize losses related to an underlying asset.

If you plan on purchasing cheap options, it is important to keep in mind that they are going to be cheap for a reason. The price is always determined by the strike price of the underlying asset combined with the amount of time remaining before the option expires. Cheap options are typically cheap because it is unlikely that they will turn a profit before they expire.

Don't ignore delta: If the delta of the option you are looking at is close to 1 then it is time to create calls, and if it is close to - 1 then it is time to create puts. If you are dealing with especially cheap options, however, then it is important to look for options with a higher delta as they are more likely to behave in an expected fashion. This, in turn, allows you to expect greater gains when the underlying asset begins to move. Different strategies are going to require different levels of the delta to be successful. Never enter into a trade without knowing where the current delta stands and how it is likely to change in your chosen timeframe.

Avoid choosing the wrong parameters: If you are working with options that deal in front month contracts, then you are going to want to keep in mind the timeframe that relates to the expectations you have regarding the underlying asset in question. While some options are always going to look good on paper, it is important not to become enamored and risk buying into a timeframe that won't provide you with enough time to turn a profit. What's more, you are always going to want to maintain a realistic set of expectations when it comes to the way the underlying asset is going to move. If you choose poorly, then you can expect a wide range of fluctuation before the option in question expires.

Not using sentiment analysis: Sentiment analysis is easy to overlook which is unfortunate because it is a reliable way to determine the likelihood that a specific trend in an underlying asset is going to continue over a set timeframe. This means you are always going to want to observe instances of short interest as well as put activity and analyst ratings to get a fair idea of underlying stock price movement in the near term. When utilizing sentiment analysis, it can be easy to mistake actual results for the mood of the market. As such you are always going to want to wait for any initial gut reaction movement to clear up before making your move.

Not taking technical indicators into account: When working with cheap options, it is important to avoid making snap judgments as they are much harder to judge accurately compared those in the midrange. This is because cheap options that represent a likely sure thing are always picked up extremely quickly so what is left requires a deeper level of analysis in order to find the best deals. Using technical indicators can then help to ensure that whatever you do, it is likely to end in your favor.

Not looking at extrinsic and intrinsic value: The extrinsic value of an option is the difference between the current price it is listed at, compared with what you are guaranteed to make off its intrinsic value or the amount its premiums will pay out, even if it expires or there is no additional movement from the underlying asset. Everyone always takes into account the intrinsic value, but the extrinsic is often left out in the cold despite still being a useful indicator. While the intrinsic value is likely to stay the same, the extrinsic value is going to decrease as the option gets closer to expiring.

Not giving commission costs proper thought: Especially if you are interested in high risk/high reward trades, not giving enough thought to your commission costs can significantly impact your overall earnings. If you chose the brokerage that you are using early on in your trading career, then there may very well be a better option out there for you. Remember, not all brokerages are created equal which means that you may very well be able to find a much better rate with only a little bit of extra research.

If you are fairly certain that you won't be able to get a better rate than what you are currently working with, then it is important that you don't waste your trading potential by working for returns that will be dramatically reduced by the fees you pay. A good rule of thumb is that you should always try to at least triple what you are paying in commission fees on every successful trade. This will ensure that you have some wiggle room for failed trades without it negatively affecting your trading capital.

Not giving enough care to your stop losses: While it is known that you should always set a stop loss on options which have a large potential for success, or those that are extremely volatile, many traders still forgo this step when the stakes are lower. While not placing a stop loss on a relatively cheap option won't lose you much by itself, getting into this habit has the potential to cost you a great deal of time. Unless you get in the habit of always protecting yourself on every trade, every time, you run the risk of burning through your trading capital much faster than you otherwise might.

Avoid trying to adapt existing strategies: While it can be easy to come to think of a successful strategy as a safety blanket, trying to use one strategy in all situations is only asking for trouble. Every time you decide to change the type of options that you target, or note that the market is changing, you will find more success by starting from scratch on an entirely new strategy than trying to shoehorn in something that no longer works as effectively as it should. While this will ultimately lead to you trading less overall, your results are sure to speak for themselves.

CHAPTER 4: ANALYZING YOUR TRADES

In order to determine if your trading system is as effective as possible, it is important to keep track of your trades and analyze the results about once a month. It is important that you don't overanalyze your results as otherwise a handful of good (or bad) trades can throw the entire average off and cause you to move forward in a less than optimal manner.

The metrics that you are going to find to be the most helpful are going to vary based on your trading style. If you prefer high risk/high reward trades, then you are going to be more interested in total net profit while if you prefer to avoid as much risk as possible, then your successful trade percentage is going to be more useful. Regardless, it is vital that you review and thoroughly understand a wide variety of different performance metrics related to your plan or your system before determining if it is time to try something new.

Performance reports: A performance report for a strategy or trading plan is an overall measurement of how it performs at the top level. A good performance report will reflect on the rules you are trading by and compares the results to an overall historical context. Also known as backtesting, this is a useful process to perform either before you begin using a new plan or once you have already started if you feel that the way it has performed so far is a fluke. Most trading platforms can generate performance reports automatically both via back testing and in real time.

The first part of any performance report is the performance summary which outlines the most important metrics of the plan or system in question. It is common for these reports to include performance graphs, trade lists, and periodical returns. They keep track of every trade that you make, the time and date it occurred, the type of trade it was along with any profits or losses that resulted from it in the form of a percentage of the cost of the trade. Remember, keeping an eye on weekly data might not be especially helpful, though quarterly or monthly data will allow you to see the forest for the trees more easily.

This information is especially helpful when you want to know not just what your trading result totals are but why specific trades played out in a specific way. When studied properly they can easily allow you to see how individual flukes can be turned into patterns. They are also useful when it comes to ensuring that you don't repeat disastrous mistakes a second time.

These details can be found in the performance graph displayed as either a bar graph that shows a monthly net profit or through what is known as an equity curve. This graph is an excellent way of gaining an overall idea of the quality of trades that are made over a given period of time without dealing with the noise inherent in the market as a whole.

Metrics to consider

Every performance report is going to include a wealth of data, much more than you are going to need in most cases. This can make getting started difficult if you don't know where to look. Consider the following metrics first and then dig deeper if you still haven't found what you are looking for.

Total net profit: The total net profit broadly determines the success or failure of a plan or system over a specific period. This number can be found by taking the total gross loss, adding it to the commission costs, and then subtracting from the total amount made from successful trades. While it is good to know if you are turning a profit, the total net profit can be deceptive as well because it won't show how often your plan or system was successful, just the overall results.

Profit factor: In order to find the profit factor of your plan or system you will want to start with the total gross profits and then divide by the total gross losses with any relevant fees added in. If the result is greater than one, then you can consider your current strategy a success. This number equates to how many units of profit you can expect for every one unit of risk you undertake. The higher the number, the greater the difference between your wins and your losses.

Profitable percentage: Also known as the probability of winning, your profitable percentage can be found by taking the number of trades that you have made successfully and dividing it by the total number of trades that you have made overall. Unlike with profit factor, there is no right answer to this amount as it is going to vary based on personal trading style. If you prefer higher risk trades, then a smaller number is acceptable. If you prefer more reliable trades, then you want the number to be as high as possible.

Trade average net profit: The trade average net profit can be thought of as how reliable your system is overall, expressed in the amount of money that typically changed hands with each trade. To find this amount all you need to do is to divide the total profit you have made by the total number of trades. If the resulting number is negative, then you know your plan needs work. When figuring out the trade average net profit, you will want to leave out any exceptionally good or bad trades as they can easily skew the results.

Chapter 5: Option Trading Strategies to Consider

While throwing yourself whole hog into the options market means taking in a great deal of information in a short period of time, there are plenty of strategies to use that are likely to improve your returns and reduce your risk as greatly as possible.

Covered call: Also called the buy-write strategy, a covered call involves purchasing an underlying asset while also generating a call on the same asset. In order to ensure this strategy works properly, it is important to create a call based around how much of the underlying asset you own. This strategy is extremely effective if you own a separate position in the short term and feel that the underlying asset is either going to stay the same or decrease in value in the time frame for the option you created. When done properly, it allows you to generate a bonus premium at the very least. Covered calls are an effective strategy when used with index futures, LEAPS and on funds that are traded via an exchange and purchased on a margin.

Married puts: To utilize a married put, the first thing you need to do is purchase a specific amount of an underlying asset before purchasing a put that covers the same amount. This should be one of your go-to strategies if you feel bullish when it comes to the price of the asset in question and are looking for an easy way to minimize losses. The put that you purchased then acts as a price floor that can help prevent a dramatic drop in price. While putting money into an asset that you believe is going to decrease in price dramatically is never recommended, if you already own the underlying asset, then a married put will help minimize future uncertainty.

While a married put isn't going to be the right choice all of the time, when used sparingly under the right conditions it can be a reliable way to increase your overall success when it comes to options trading. To ensure that it always works out in your favor you are going to want to begin each transaction with a clear understanding of the risk in question. You can then factor in the added costs of a married put compared to the mitigation of that risk to determine if it is worth moving forward. As an added bonus, married puts help mitigate the potential risk related to early options to exercise as it ensures you always have available shares ready and waiting.

Bull call spread: To use this strategy, you will want to start by purchasing a call option at a strike price you believe to be beneficial. You will then want to sell a similar number of calls at a higher strike price. Both calls should have the same underlying asset and the same timeframe. This is a useful strategy to use if you are bullish on the strength of the underlying asset in question and your research indicates that the price is likely to increase in the time frame you have chosen.

This strategy is also known as a vertical credit spread because it has a pair of mismatched legs. Legs that are sold close to the money generate a credit spread that typically contains a net credit along with a positive time value. On the other hand, a debit spread is created with a short option that ends further from the money than when it started. Overall, this strategy is considered a net buy.

Bear put spread: The bear put spread is similar to the bull call spread but is used in opposite circumstances. Specifically, you begin by purchasing a pair of put options, one at a higher strike price and another at a lower strike price. You are going to want to purchase an equal number of each and ensure that they have the same underlying asset and timeframe. This strategy is useful when you feel bearish on the underlying asset in question as it helps you limit your losses if you are incorrect about the way the market is moving. This strategy should be used cautiously, however, as your overall profits are going to be limited to the difference between the two puts you purchased minus the cost of any transaction fees.

The ideal time to use a bear put spread is if you are interested in short selling an underlying asset and using a more common put option doesn't seem to be the right choice. You will find them useful if you are interested in speculating that prices are on a downward trend and don't want to invest a larger amount of capital waiting for the worst to happen. When using a bear put spread you are literally planning for the worst while hoping for the best.

Protective collar: To use the protective collar strategy you are going to want to start by purchasing a put option that is currently out of the money. You will then want to write a different call option based on the same underlying asset that is also out of the money. This is an ideal strategy to use when you have a long position on an underlying asset that has seen significant gains in the recent past. Using a protective collar allows you to both ensure the current level of profit while also holding onto the underlying asset in case it continues to increase in value.

Using a protective collar is as simple as placing the contract for the put option you purchased at a strike price that guarantees you hold on to a majority of the profit you have made. After that, you will be able to fund the collar strategy with the call option that you have written, making sure that it relates to a specific Digit. This strategy is a great way to maintain your profits while adding very little to your overall costs. What's more, it is very easy to ensure that you don't have to pay any related taxes as you can allow the option to roll over for as long as you deem necessary.

Straddles: The long straddle strategy is most useful after you have already purchased both a put and a call that share the same timeframe, underlying asset and strike price. It is useful if you believe that the price of the underlying asset is going to move significantly in one direction, you just don't know which direction it is going to be. Putting a long straddle into effect allows you to rest easy as you will see a gain as long as the price starts moving within the time frame you have chosen.

Alternatively, to institute a short straddle, you will want to sell a call and a put with the same timeframe, the same costs and related to the same underlying asset. This will ensure that you make a profit from the premium if you don't expect the underlying asset to move much in either direction in the specified timeframe. Be aware, however, that the odds of success will decrease proportionally to the amount that the underlying asset moves in the given timeframe.

Long strangle: In order to utilize a long strangle you will want to purchase both a put and a call that use the same underlying asset and share a maturation level. They are also going to need different strike prices. The strike price for the put should be somewhat lower than the price of the call, and both should be at a point out of the money. This is a useful strategy if you expect the underlying asset to move significantly but are unsure of the direction it will take. When used properly, you are virtually guaranteed a profit minus any related costs.

A strangle functions much like a straddle except that it tends to be cheaper as you are purchasing options that are already out of the money. This means you can routinely expect to pay as much as 50 percent less which makes it easier to play both sides of the fence. When given the option, a long strangle is preferable to a short straddle as it offers the chance at twice the premium while forcing you to take on the same amount of risk.

Butterfly spread: A butterfly spread requires the use of a bear spread strategy in addition to a bull strategy and contains three separate strike points. To start you want to purchase a call option at the lowest price you can manage. You will then want to sell two calls at a higher price and a third call at a price that is higher still. Your goal is to ensure a range of potential profits at prices you believe will be profitable. The most effective time to use a butterfly spread is when you have a neutral opinion on the current state of the market.

It is a good idea to utilize a butterfly spread when you expect the underlying asset that you favor to increase in price but are unsure of how much gain to expect. As such, you are going to want to make sure the overall market volatility is as low as possible. The higher the overall level of volatility, the more setting up a butterfly spread will cost you. The butterfly spread is not without a downside, however, as if you are wrong about the direction the underlying asset is going to move in then the losses can be significant.

Iron Condor: In order to use the iron condor strategy, you are going to want to start with a short position and a long position utilizing a pair of 'strangle' strategies to take full advantage of a market that is low in volatility. One 'strangle' is going to be long and the other short and set to an outer strike price. You can also move forward using two credit spreads. In this case, the call spread would be above the current market price, and the put would be below the current market price.

You are only going to want to attempt the iron condor when trading in index options because they offer a unique mix of increased volatility coupled with a lower increase in risk. Additionally, it is important to put an iron condor into play only when you are extremely confident you know where the market is going. This is because the potential for loss, should you choose poorly, is very great. Assuming all goes according to plan you then stand to make a significant profit assuming the market doesn't move strongly in one direction or the other.

Iron Butterfly: To start an iron butterfly you want to use either a long or a short straddle and concurrently either purchase or sell a strangle based on the straddle you chose. While similar to a basic butterfly, this strategy utilizes both calls and puts rather than just one or the other. When done properly it limits the potential for profit or loss to the range of the strike prices that you set. This strategy is best used with options that are out of the money as they allow you to minimize both risk and cost.

The pair of options that you use in the iron butterfly should be set at a mid-strike point to generate either a short or a long straddle depending on if you are buying or selling. The so-called wings of the butterfly are formed from the pair of options at the lower strike price and the higher strike price that are generated once the strangle is sold. This helps to offset the long or short position which creates the limits regarding your total profits or losses.

CHAPTER 6: ADVANCED STRATEGIES TO TRY

Double diagonal strategy: In order to properly use the double diagonal strategy, you will start with a diagonal put spread along with a diagonal call spread. You can turn a horizontal spread into a diagonal spread by simply shifting the long leg to a new strike point with a different timeframe. Any spread where the two legs don't use the same month is said to be diagonal.

When using a diagonal call spread, you will need to combine a short call spread and a long calendar spread to allow it to move based on the rate at which time decay affects the option in question. Once you sell off the second call at the initial strike point, you will have backed into a spread for the short call. This will allow you to create a net credit which means that after the second call has been sold anything else you make is pure profit. A diagonal put works in largely the same way with the specifics reversed.

144

To run a double diagonal, you will start by putting a diagonal put spread and a diagonal call spread into play. This will provide you with the opportunity to profit from the increased time decay that front-month options experience when compared with back-month options.

To do so, you start with buying a put that is currently out of the money at a strike price that will be good for two months. At the same time, you will want to sell an out of the money put at a strike price that is good for one month. Furthermore, you are going to want to sell a call that is out of the money at a strike price that is good for one month. Finally, you will purchase a call at a separate strike price that is good for two months.

If everything goes according to plan, then the underlying asset will remain at a price that is between the second put and the first call. If the price remains above that pair of strike prices, then you are going to want to sell the options that are one month out. At the same time, you are going to want to sell another call with the same strike price as the call that is two months out.

When graphing this strategy, it is important to keep in mind that the profit and loss lines are not going to be as straight as you might expect because the two month options are still growing concerns. Straight lines and hard angles can only exist if the options you are graphing are all going to expire in the same timeframe.

While this strategy might seem extremely complicated at first, it can be made to seem much more manageable if you instead consider it as a form of profiting from a neutral amount of movement in the market, simply spread out into multiple expiration cycles.

The most useful time to use this strategy is when an underlying asset is halfway between the second put and the first call, the closer to the true midpoint the better. If the underlying asset isn't at this point, then biases towards bullishness or bearishness can skew the results. If the underlying asset remains at the midpoint, then the options you sold will expire without generating a profit, allowing you to keep a greater percentage of the premium.

This occurs because the first put and the second call that you purchased will help to decrease your overall risk, even if the underlying asset moves more than you might like. The goal of this strategy is to leave you with a net credit, though this is not always how things shake out. It is not a sure thing because the front month trades inherently have less time value which means that a net debit is a possibility. If this occurs, then you can make up the difference by selling the remaining options after the front month pair expires.

When the front month pair is close to expiring, and the price of the underlying asset is somewhere between the price of the second put and the first call then you are going to way to buy close to the pair of puts and create an additional put for sale at the second strike price along with a third call at the third strike price. These new options should have the same expiration as the other two month options. This is what is known as rolling out, and it can easily double, or even triple, your profits.

Leveraged covered call strategy: Also known as the fig leaf strategy, the leveraged covered call strategy is a great way to mitigate some of the risks that come along with trading options based on Long Term Equity Anticipation Securities

(LEAPS). A standard LEAPS call is not set to expire for at least a year which means a short-term call lasts about 45 days. This strategy is useful if you feel somewhat bullish about the market's chances over this timeframe.

To utilize this strategy, you are going to start by purchasing a LEAPS call with access to a profitable strike price for the related underlying asset. At the same time, you are going to sell a call at a favorable strike price to ensure you can make a profit if you end up being assigned early. The goal here is to provide a covered call for the LEAPS transaction. While the two options you have committed two are similar, the fact that they have different expiration dates allows you to maximize your profits when compared with a standard covered call. Next, you are going to sell a call that is out of the money in the short term at the same strike price as the call. Ideally, the underlying asset will then stick close to the second strike price and not the first.

This strategy is useful if you don't want to put up all of the required capital right at the start. This, in turn, means that the premium that is generated as you sell the call is going to represent a larger percentage of your initial investment, leverage will ensure your profits are proportionally higher as well.

When graphing this strategy, be aware that your loss and profit lines will not be straight as the LEAPS call is going to remain open while the other call expires. You should also keep in mind that determining what your likely profits are going to be is tricky, in this instance, because the available data won't be reliable until enough time has passed to see where the LEAPs call is likely to end up.

When using the fig leaf strategy, your goal should be to purchase a LEAPS call that is going to move in the same way as the underlying asset. As such, it is recommended that you only consider calls that have a delta of .8 or higher. This means you are going to want to look at options that are at least 20 percent of the money. If you are considering an underlying asset that experiences a high degree of volatility, then options that are at least 40 percent of the money are recommended.

While this strategy is more useful in many situations than a traditional covered call, it is not with additional risks. First, unlike most underlying assets, LEAPS eventually expire which is something you need to take into account if you are to keep your investment. Second, being assigned on the short call can be cumbersome as you likely won't own the underlying asset when it occurs. You won't want to exercise your option to buy on the LEAPS call because you lose out on a significant amount of time value. The best solution is simply to hope that the short call expires out of the money and that you can sell it multiple times before the LEAPS call ultimately expires. Alternatively, you can sell the LEAPS call on the open market to ensure that you profit from the time value that remains. If you go this route, you are going to want to ensure that you also purchase the underlying asset to cover any short positions that might materialize.

This is an effective strategy if you have a clear idea of how an underlying asset is going to move but cannot currently afford to purchase it directly. If the price of this assets jumps the first strike price and heads right toward the second, then you can make an early profit by closing out the whole option.

Skip strike butterfly call spread: The biggest difference between a skip strike butterfly call spread and a traditional butterfly spread is that is much more directionally focused. With the skip strike version, you are going to want the underlying stock price to increase, though not beyond the limit of your secondary strike price. The calls at the second and fourth strike points will be nearly 0 though you will still retain the premium generated by the call at the primary strike price.

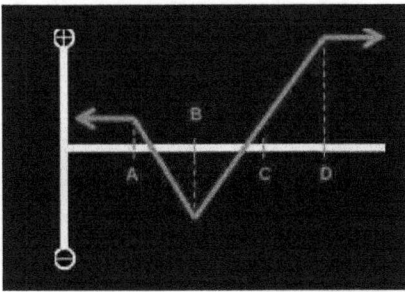

This strategy works by placing a short call spread into a butterfly long call spread. Essentially what you are doing is unloading the short call spread as a means of paying for the butterfly. While this would technically mean that you need to buy and sell a call at the same strike price, the results of this transaction would balance out so it can be skipped.

The spread on the short call allows for this strategy to be arranged with little extra cost in exchange for the chance at a significant gain. This also adds risk to the proceedings making the skip strike butterfly call spread riskier than a traditional butterfly spread. In order to get the best results from this strategy, you are going to want to ensure that all of the strike prices that you use are equidistance from one another while also expiring in the same month. The price of the underlying asset in question should then remain at or below the first strike price for the best results.

To use the skip strike butterfly call spread the first thing you are going to want to do is to purchase a call at the primary strike point. You will then want to sell a pair of calls at the second strike price. Finally, you are going to want to ignore the third strike price and purchase a call at the fourth strike price.

This is a terrific strategy to use if you are primarily interested in minimizing risk. This is the case because the underlying asset would need to see significant movement before breaking past the strike point for you to see serious losses. The risk with this strategy can be further mitigated if you utilize it with options based on indices instead of stocks because many indices experience very low volatility as conflicting internal price movements often cancel one another out.

This strategy is especially effective if you are bullish about the state of the market as it currently stands and where it is likely to go in the time frame that you have established. As long as you hit the third strike price, you can expect to make a profit even if the options are going to expire at a point that would traditionally allow you to break even. In order to make the maximum amount of profit, you would want to exercise the moment the underlying asset reaches the second strike price. You will then make a profit based on the second strike price subtracted by the first and any related fees.

Skip strike butterfly put spread: Much like the skip strike butterfly call spread, the put version skews more towards a directional strategy than the butterfly spread version. The biggest difference between the two is that while the traditional version hopes for the underlying asset to increase, the skip strike version hopes for the underlying asset to decrease in value, though not beyond the third strike price you have established.

As such, this is a good strategy to use if you are a little bearish on the state of the market as you will not want the underlying asset to decrease too far. If things work out as they should, you would then make no profit off of the first and second put, but you will earn a premium on the fourth put. This strategy works by establishing a short put spread inside a butterfly put spread that has a longer timeframe. Much like with the call variant, you can avoid buying and selling at the second strike point as these actions will cancel one another out. Furthermore, the short spread will provide you with the opportunity to use this strategy as a way to generate either a small debit or a positive credit. Like its counterpart, the skip strike butterfly put is riskier than the standard butterfly variation, though the potential for return is greater as well.

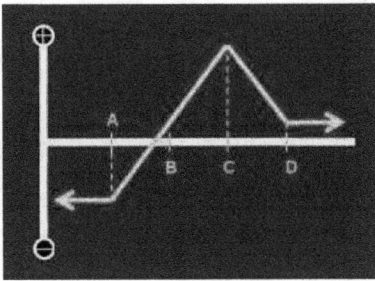

To start using this strategy, you will first purchase a put at the primary strike price. The second strike point can then be skipped as the two purchases cancel one another out. Next, you will purchase two puts at the third strike price. Finally, you will purchase a put at the fourth strike price. All the strike prices need to be equidistance from one another and have the same expiration month. For the best results, you will want the underlying asset price to remain at or above the third strike price.

In order to make as much as possible from this strategy, you are going to want to execute the moment the underlying asset reaches the third strike price. The maximum amount of profit from this strategy is limited to the difference between the final two strike prices, minus any additional fees. In order to break even with this strategy, and still generate a credit, you will need the underlying asset to remain at or above the secondary strike price. On the other hand, if the trade was set up to generate a net debit then you will be able to break even at the fourth strike price as well as the second.

CONCLUSION

Thank for making it through to the end of *Options Trading: The Ultimate Guide to Options Trading*, let's hope it was informative and able to provide you with all of the tools you need to achieve your financial goals, whatever it is that they may be. Just because you've finished this book doesn't mean there is nothing left to learn on the topic, expanding your horizons is the only way to find the mastery you seek.

The next step is to stop reading already and to get ready to start trading options as effectively as possible. With the strategies and tips provided in the preceding chapters, you should have the tools you need to be successful regardless of the current state of the market. This isn't a sure thing, however, and only by taking the time to truly analyze not only the current state of the market but also the current and likely future state of the options you are interested in can you maximize your trade percentage as completely as possible.

While it can be difficult to know the right move early on in your trading career, if you trust yourself throughout, then eventually that trust will be justified.

Just because you are now armed with everything you need to trade options successfully, doesn't mean that you can expect the profits to start rolling in right away. It is important to keep the right mindset, day in and day out if you hope to be a successful options trader in the long term. No matter how good you are, major windfalls are rare and chasing them is only going to cause your trading capital to dwindle. It is always going to be a better choice to take solid, reliable profits over riskier alternatives; remember options trading is a marathon, not a sprint, slow and steady wins the race.

Finally, if you found this book useful in any way, a review on Amazon is always appreciated!

OPTIONS TRADING: STRATEGIES ON HOW TO EXCEL AT OPTIONS TRADING

DESCRIPTION

When it comes to having a little wiggle room in the stock market, options trading can't be beaten. The simple ability to choose whether or not you want to purchase the underlying stock attached to your options can easily lead to success in scenarios that would only lead to failure in the stock market. With that being said, however, in order to maximize your options trading experience, you need to be able to rely on successful strategies you can count on when the going gets tough. If you are looking to take your options trading game to the next level, then *Options Trading: Strategies on How to Excel at Options Trading* is the book that you have been waiting for.

Inside you will find over a dozen different strategies that can be used regardless of the market conditions or if you are selling or buying, and often both at once. You will find strategies that cover multiple types of spreads, notes for trading indices, the weekly options market, how to minimize an existing bad trade via the stock repair strategy and more.

Without a doubt, this book contains everything you need in order to stop questioning potential trades and start acting in a manner that will ensure you maximize your profits with every trade. After all, time is always of the essence when it comes to making the best trades and *Options Trading: Strategies on How to Excel at Options Trading* will get you to the place you need to be to stop second-guessing and start succeeding. No matter what level of risk you prefer or how long you have been in the options market, you will find something useful inside.

So, what are you waiting for? The options market is all about choice and now is the time to choose to stop wasting time on trades that do little more than break even. Take control of your trade experience and buy this book today!

Inside you will find

- The best time to utilize the index straddle and why you may want to consider options trading in the indices in general.

- The best way to break even on stocks that have already dropped out of the money.

- Spreads, spreads and more spreads. Nearly ten different spread strategies to ensure you have the right spread for every occasion.

- The top technical indicators for the options market that you likely aren't already using.

- The complete details on the little-known options trading market that is perfect for short term trades.

- All about combination strategies and why you need to start using them right now.

- *And more...*

INTRODUCTION

Congratulations on downloading *Options Trading: Strategies on How to Excel at Options Trading* and thank you for doing so. When it comes to having a little wiggle room in the stock market, options trading can't be beaten. The simple ability to choose whether or not you want to purchase the underlying stock attached to your options can easily lead to success in scenarios that would only lead to failure in the stock market. With that being said, however, in order to maximize your options trading experience, you need to be able to rely on successful strategies you can count on when the going gets tough.

To that end, the following chapters will discuss a wide variety of different options trading strategies designed to ensure that your time spent trading options is as fruitful and painless as possible. First, you will learn all about long and short combinations as well as when the best time to use each

166

really is. Next, you will learn how to put straddles to use in the index market as well as the benefits of trading options in the index market in general. From there you will learn how to minimize the impact of a bad stock trade via the stock repair strategy.

Then you will learn how to use both vertical and horizontal spread strategies before learning all the details of ratio and front spread strategies as well. The talk of spread strategies then wraps up with a detailed discussion of both put and call backspread strategies. Up next you will learn about many of the technical indicators that work best with options trading and why you will always want to use multiple indicators no matter what. Finally, things will wrap up with a discussion of the pros and cons of weekly options trading and why it may be the right choice for you.

There are plenty of books on this subject on the market, thanks again for choosing this one! Every effort was made to ensure it is full of as much useful information as possible, please enjoy!

CHAPTER 1: COMBINATION STRATEGIES

Long combination

Also known as the synthetic long stock strategy, the long combination is utilized by purchasing a call and a put with the same details at the same strike price. You will want the underlying asset price to be quite close to the strike price when you pull the trigger. This is a bullish strategy, and the short put is uncovered which leaves you with a significant amount of risk if things go wrong. As such, this strategy is only recommended when the indicators you favor show that the market is likely to move in the way you expect.

This strategy is known as the synthetic long stock due to the fact that the risk and reward are nearly the same as the more common long stock strategy. Additionally, if you hold onto the position until it expires you will likely end up purchasing the underlying asset anyway. Specifically, if the underlying

169

asset ends up higher than the strike price, then you will want to exercise the call. Meanwhile, if it is below the strike price, it is very likely that the put will be assigned which means you will still need to purchase the asset.

With that being said, there is no limit to how much you want the underlying asset to move once you have set up this strategy, the more positive momentum it has, the more money you stand to make. The maximum amount you can expect to lose if things don't go according to plan is limited to the amount of the strike price plus the net debit or minus the net credit.

In this case, purchasing the call will give you the right to purchase the underlying asset at the strike price. Selling the put at the same price then obligates you to purchase the underlying asset at this price if you find yourself in a situation where the option is assigned.

Time decay is a relatively neutral factor for this strategy. On the other hand, it will erode the value of the purchased option which is far from ideal. On the other hand, it will also decrease the value of the option being sold. Likewise, the implied volatility of this option is fairly neutral as well. It will increase the value of the option being sold while doing the same to the option being purchased.

While on paper this strategy might not seem more beneficial than simply purchasing the underlying asset directly, the fact of the matter is that the leverage in play makes it worthwhile to purchase the option instead. Specifically, this way you get all of the same benefits as purchasing directly while still allowing your money to work for you in other capacities until the option expires.

Furthermore, when you first start this strategy, you will have additional requirements when it comes to margin due to the short put. You will also need to pay a net debit in order to establish the position. These costs will still be relatively small compared to the upfront price of the underlying asset.

When utilizing this strategy, it is important to be aware that the price of the underlying asset is rarely going to sit precisely at the strike price. If this price is above the strike price, then the call will typically cost more than the put which means you will start with a greater net debit. The opposite is also true and will result in a net credit.

Carry costs and dividends will also come into play with this strategy. As an example, if a company that previously never paid dividends suddenly started up this practice then the prices of both calls and puts are sure to change. This will occur due to the fact that the underlying stock price will be expected to drop by the amount of the dividend right after the dividend is paid. This, in turn, will cause the price of puts to increase and the price of calls to decrease before the stock price drops due to the anticipation of the decrease. As such, if the put cost exceeds the call cost then you will be able to use this strategy with a net credit.

Short combination

Also known as the synthetic short stock, this strategy is put into effect by purchasing a put and a call at the same strike price with the same characteristics. The best time to pursue this strategy is when the underlying asset is close to the strike price. As with the long combination, this strategy has the potential for great risk. However, also like the long combination there is no limit to how much you want the underlying asset to move as the further down it goes the greater your opportunity for profit is going to be.

The amount you can expect to make on the strategy is determined by the amount the underlying asset moves from the strike price minus any debits or adding any credits that were generated during its creation. If you hold onto the position until it reaches the point of expiration you are almost always going to end up selling either because the call has been assigned or because it is a good value.

In this instance, both time decay and implied volatility are going to remain mostly neutral. This is the case because it affects both sides of the strategy in equal amounts.

When starting this strategy, you are going to receive a net credit most of the time, but there will also be some margin requirements due to the short call. These costs are going to be relatively small when compared to the amount that you could make the trade, however. One of the number one reasons this strategy is used is that it doesn't require much cash to be held up via margin when creating the short stock position.

It is also important to keep in mind potential changes to the price based on dividends as they will determine if this strategy can be established for a net debit or a net credit. However, this is a useful strategy if you own a particular stock that you plan on shorting and that stock has a pending dividend. Typically, if you are short stock, then you will have to pay the dividends from your own account, but if you use this strategy, that requirement will not apply.

CHAPTER 2: INDEX STRADDLES

Purchasing an index straddle requires you to buy an index put and an index call from the same index, with the same strike price and expiration month. A long straddle position is frequently obtained and then sold at the same time in an effort to generate a larger profit or minimize loss. In this strategy, as long as you hold both the put as well as the call then your investment is hedged. This is due to the fact that the call has the potential to increase in value as the index rises and the put have the potential to increase in value as the value of the index decreases.

Purchasing an index straddle provides you with the benefits of both the index call and the index put. It also leverages the profit potential when the underlying index moves significantly in either direction from the entry point. Alternately, those who purchase straddles may instead focus on short-term gains when the volatility levels change despite a lack of significant movement from the related index. This typically leads to smaller, more reliable profits. Regardless of the path you choose, the amount of risk you run will be both predetermined and limited.

You should consider purchasing an index straddle if you are fairly confident the index is going to move in a big way, but you don't know if that move will be up or down. It is also a fine choice if you expect the volatility of the index to increase both up and down near the current level while at the same time expecting an increase in the implied volatility of the overlying options. Finally, it is ideal if you prefer a limited amount of risk but would still prefer to utilize the added leverage that options provide.

As with any long index trade, the options holder always has the opportunity to exercise the option prior to, or at the point of, its expiration. Additionally, the option can be sold in the marketplace as they almost always retain their market value throughout a greater portion of the time prior to their expiration.

This strategy is not especially bearish or bullish but instead is a combination of the two. The potential for profit of the long call at the point of expiration can be quite large as long as the underlying index continues to increase past the initial breakeven point. Likewise, the long put has the same potential assuming the related index continues to decrease steadily from the starting point. The long index straddle is only limited by the momentum of the movement, not the movement itself.

This strategy has two separation breakeven points for when the options expire. The upside breakeven point is equal to the contract of the underlying index level's strike price plus any premiums paid for the put and the call. The downside breakeven point is the index level that is equal to the strike price minus the cost of the call and the premium on the put.

Volatility increases are positive for this strategy while lowered volatility has a negative effect that is more prevalent that either the basic put or long call due to the dual nature of the strategy. Regardless, time decay will always have a negative effect on this strategy.

Index straddle example

A good example of the right time to utilize an index straddle is as follows. For the sake of this example assume the Federal Reserve has let it be known that it is considering raising the Fed Funds rate in an effort to combat inflation.

This decision will go into effect next month and was influenced primarily by producer and consumer price data that will be made available to the public in the interim. An increase in the interest rate would likely cause index prices to decrease sharply. Maintaining the status quo may boost them to record highs. All told the market is likely to move in one direction or the other by 5 percent or more in the month following the announcement.

With this information in hand, let's say that you are interested in a specific index that is currently sitting at 100. You would then purchase a one-month call (assume the current cost is $1.70) and a put (assume the rate is $1.50). The total cost for the index straddle strategy is then $3.20 multiplied by 100 for a total of $320. By making this purchase, you are indicating that you anticipate the index is going to move beyond one of the breakeven points.

In this scenario, the upside breakeven point would be $3.20 plus the 100 strike price for a total of $103.20. The downside breakeven point would be 100-$3.20 for a total of $96.80. The potential for profit in this situation is essentially unlimited assuming the price of the index increases to a point above 103.20 or drops below 96.80 before the expiration date. The risk for this strategy is set at the premium of $320 and would only come into play if the price of the index doesn't move at all, staying at 100 for the entire month.

If the price moves in enough of a positive or negative direction, then you would be free to sell both the call and the put in the open marketplace to take advantage of the gain. However, if things don't change enough to realize the profit, then it is likely that you would have to sell at a loss thanks to the effect of time decay.

If the index ends up closes at a point above the 103.2 breakeven point (at 105 for this example), then the put is going to expire out of the money and end up being worthless. The call will be on the money, however, which means it will be worth its intrinsic value which can be determined by the difference between the index level and its strike price. In this case, it would be $105-$100 for a gain of $5 per share or $500 in this scenario. The same would be true if the put expires in the money and the call expires worthlessly. The total profit is then tallied by subtracting $3.20 from $5 for a profit of $1.80 or 180 on 100 shares.

The biggest risk in this instance is if the index doesn't change at all, leaving the price at $100 and ensuring a total loss of the initial $320 investment. Meanwhile, if the index moved upwards to 102, then the put would expire worthlessly and out of the money while the call would have an intrinsic value of $2 per share which, while still a positive amount, is not enough movement to actually turn a profit. The best course of action in this scenario would still be to sell, however, as you will be able to recoup more than half of your losses.

Instead of being motivated purely by the potential price movement, you could instead be motivated by how much you expect the volatility of a given index to change over the predetermined period. In this case, assume that at the start of the 30 days the index had a volatility level of 14 percent and after 10 days it has already increased to 19 percent. With this information, you can then determine what the likely amount of profit is going to be at the end of the 30 days.

You can then expect the call to be at an expected value of $1.85 (up from $1.70) and the put to have an expected value of $1.70 (up from $1.50). This would then indicate that the expected value at the end of the 30 days would be about $3.50 which is enough to turn a $30 profit when it expires. While not great, it is practically guaranteed which means that it can be used to offset extra costs associated with riskier trades. This $30 then represent a return of 9.4 percent in just 10 days.

When you hold onto an index straddle for the purpose of waiting for an anticipated volatility increase, you are in a sense protected from large movements that may happen suddenly. In fact, if the index level ends up moving dramatically while you are on the hook for the index sample you can even make a profit on the value of the put or the call without any increase in the implied volatility.

CHAPTER 3: STOCK REPAIR STRATEGY

This is a great strategy to employ if you have already purchased shares of stock that are optionable and are stuck in a situation where you are watching its value decline with no clear recourse to rectify the situation. If the stock you purchased was non-actionable, then all you would be able to do is hold onto it in hopes that things turn around or double down in hopes of turning a profit at a lower breakeven point. Luckily, with optionable stocks, you also have a third alternative.

The stock repair strategy is ideal for those who are looking to break even on a stock that they purchased at a point significantly higher than where the current market price stands and are looking to break even. It is important to keep in mind that you will need to be willing to forfeit any profit potential, even at the reduced breakeven point. This is also a

185

good choice if you can't or are unwilling to commit any additional funds to the position in question.

The repair strategy is useful in helping you break even, especially if you are already in losing position. To utilize it you are going to want to sell 2 call options at a strike price above the current stock price and purchase 1 call option at the current price for every 100 shares of the failing stock you own. All of the options should have the same period of expiration. These sales and purchases are constructed in such a way that the additional funds you have to invest are slim to none.

Stock repair example

As an example, consider that you started out with 100 shares of a stock that you purchased for $50 a piece only to watch them fall to the current price of $40 each. You are unwilling to invest anything else into this stock and are afraid to take any more downside risk. Once you are ready simply to break even, then it is time to initiate the stock repair strategy.

To begin, you would want to purchase a single 60-day call option on the stock at the $40 price point for $3 while also selling 2 60-day call options at $1.50. It is important to keep in mind that the spread won't cost you any credits or debits. This is because the cost of the calls you purchased at the rate of $3 per 100 shares for a total of $300, will be completely offset by the premium that is generated from the sale of the written calls at the rate of $1.50x2x100 for a total of $300.

The purchase of the $40 call will provide you with the opportunity to purchase another 100 shares at the $40 price point while the 2 $45 calls will mean that you have to sell 200 shares at $45 if you are assigned. While you currently only have 100 shares, you could exercise the $40 long call to generate the required extra shares and make $5 per share at a relative profit of $500 which would cover the assignment.

There are several different likely scenarios that will come into play at the point the options expire. First, the underlying stock could continue to decrease and close around $35. It could remain at the current rate and close at $40. It could also regain some lost ground and close at $45. The best-case scenario is that it rises back to the price purchase price of $50 per share.

If the underlying stock continues to decrease in value and ends at $35, then all 3 of the calls will expire worthlessly out of the money. As the option position didn't cost anything to execute you wouldn't be out any more money that you would if you had simply held the stock and waited to see what would happen. As such the strategy has no negative or positive effect. This illustrates a salient point that this strategy will do nothing to protect you from additional losses to the underlying stocks. As such, if you expect the price to continue to fall after the initial decrease then a different strategy is recommended.

If the underlying stock remains at the $40 price point until the options expire then all of the call options will expire without any value. Once again, nothing extra was lost in the construction of the strategy, and you would be in the same position from where you started. If nothing else has changed, setting up a new round of calls and attempting the strategy again is recommended.

If the underlying stock rises in value to the point that is only $5 less than when you first purchased it then the short calls at the $45 price point will expire without value. However, the long call can then be sold at a $5 profit per share as the strategy was implemented with no additional costs. This, in turn, will reduce the amount lost on the original price decline to just $5 per share instead of $10 per share. After the $5 profit is factored in you will actually break even via this occurrence. Essentially what is managed in this scenario is that you have lowered the initial breakeven point from $50 to $45, breaking even without requiring the underlying stock to recover past the original purchase price.

If the price of the underlying stock rallies back to the original price of $50 per share then the long shares will be in a breakeven position, the long call at $40 will be worth $10, and the short calls will now be worth -$5 each. The net result of this will be that you still breakeven overall with the gains and the losses canceling one another out. Even if the price continues to rise past the $50 point, you will still be unable to make a profit as the mixture of calls will continue to cancel one another out.

As such, if you feel as though there is a chance that the underlying stock is going to rally, then in order to mitigate the constant breakeven status you would want to liquidate the new positions you created as quickly as possible. You could sell the $40 call for the intrinsic value it holds of $10 and purchase the $45 calls for their intrinsic value of $5 and close out the strategy for just the added commission costs. With this done you would then be left free and clear on your 100 shares and once again able to profit from prices increases past the original $50.

Determine the right strike price

One of the most important considerations that come along with establishing a repair strategy that can be as effective as possible is determining the right option to purchase and the correct one to sell. The $5 price chosen in the above example took half of the unrealized loss into account. As such, if you started with an underlying stock priced at $100 and were currently sitting with shares at $90 then you would want to purchase calls at $90 and sell calls at $100 as $10 is half the unrealized loss. If you plan on purchasing at the money options, then you will want to sell out of the money options that are halfway between the current price of the underlying stock and the price you originally paid.

Furthermore, it is important to keep in mind that the repair strategy will not work successfully for every stock that is currently trading below the purchase price. The strategy tends to be effective for stocks that are down up to 20 percent from their original purchase point as long as options are utilized with a range of between 60 and 90 days. However, it is ineffective if the underlying stock has already dropped as much as 40 or 50 percent. In these cases, the selling of a pair of out of the money calls will not make up the difference and generate a large enough premium to balance out the cost of the single at the money call.

Finally, it is important to keep in mind that the stock repair strategy can often be initiated for a small debit or credit. You may still want to consider it a viable strategy if you have to pay up to $.50 for initiating the position. If this is the case, then you will need to give up a small debit regardless of how high the underlying stock will ultimately increase in price. However, the effectiveness of the strategy may still outweigh these additional costs.

On the other hand, however, if the option position is established for a credit that is slightly above the break-even point then you might keep the credit. The final loss or profit scenarios use this strategy will then vary depending on the original price of the underlying stock when it was purchased, the price of the stock when the repair strategy was put into play, whether a debit or credit was required to establish the position and the strike prices chosen.

CHAPTER 4: VERTICAL AND HORIZONTAL SPREAD STRATEGIES

Spread options trading strategies are useful in a wide variety of market conditions including bearish, neutral and bullish. Essentially, they function by limiting risk at the cost of limiting profits as well. Spread trading is defined as opening a position by selling and buying multiples of either puts or calls at the same time. If you buy a put or a call while also selling another put or a call with many of the same defining characteristics, then you can consider yourself a spread trader.

This strategy limits risk as you will always know the difference between the strike prices or the expiration dates of the given options. This difference is often referred to as the spread which gives this type of strategy its name.

Vertical spread

A vertical spread is a type of spread option where the 2 options you purchased, one to sell and one to buy, have the same expiration date and a different strike price. As an example, if you purchase one $60 option for stock A and sell a $70 option for stock A then you will have generated a vertical spread. To understand the benefits of this strategy, consider the following example.

Assume you own an underlying stock that is currently valued at $50 which you expect to rise a modest amount to $55. In order to take advantage of this opportunity, you are going to want to start a vertical spread. To do so, you purchase a $50 call option while at the same time selling a call option for $55. The $50 call is in the money which means it has a $1 premium while the $55 call has a $.25 premium as it is $5 out of the money. You would then pay $1 for the $50 call and earn $.25 on the $55 call, so the entire strategy costs you $.75 to set up.

From this point, one of two things can happen. The stock can either increase in price as you assumed it would, or it can drop below the current price and take you by surprise. Assume that you made a poor prediction and the price dropped from $50 to $45. Both the calls will then expire out of the money, and you don't need to do anything but close the position out of the money. The loss in this instance would be just $.75.

On the contrary, if the price did what you expected and rose to $55 then the $50 call would now be in the money for $5 which means it has a premium of $6. The $55 call is also now in the money and will also have a premium of $1. You cannot simply wait until the option expires in this scenario because the call you sold is now a naked call which is a call that is not currently covered by stocks you own. As such, you will need to close your position before the options expire to protect your position.

This means you will need to sell the $50 call for a profit while buying back the $55 call that was sold earlier. You would then want to sell the call for $6 and purchase the other call for $1. This transaction will then have earned you $4.25 total net gain once the $1 profit and the cost of the transaction have both been taken into account.

While this is all well and good, if, instead, the price jumps to $60 instead of $66 then the limited profit side of the equation comes in along with the limited risk. If the current price is $60, then the $50 call would be in the money to $10 which means it has an $11 premium. The $55 call would then be on the money as well and have a $6 premium. If you choose to close this position out at this time, then you would still make $5 overall, and $4.25 after fees are taken into account.

Once both of the calls have made it to in the money status, then the total profit is always going to be limited by the difference of the pair of strike prices after all the fees have been taken into account. In general, after the value of the underlying stock reaches the lower call you will start to earn a profit. Once it reaches past the higher call, then the maximum amount of profit has been reached.

Regardless of the fact that the potential for profit is limited, the fact that it costs less to execute than a traditional call option makes it worthwhile in cases where you do not believe the price of the underlying stock is going to move very much. This strategy is ideal for stocks that are currently experiencing a period of moderate bullishness.

Horizontal Spread

Also known as time spreads or calendar spreads, horizontal spreads are a type of spread where the strike price of the pair of options stays the same but the time in which they expire is different. All options have a time value associated with their costs. As time goes by, an option's premium typically begins to lose value based on the amount of time it has left as it is less likely to turn a profit in the shorter remaining time period. Additionally, the closer the expiration date looms the greater the decrease in value that can be expected. The horizontal spread uses the premium decay to your advantage.

As an example, assume that you are currently in the middle of the month of June when you decide to use a horizontal spread on an underlying stock. Assume the strike price of an option expiring in August is $4 while the strike price of the option that expires in September is $4.50.

To initiate this spread, you would want to sell the August option as it is the nearer of the two and then buy the option that is farther out (September in this case). As such you would earn $4 on the sale of the first option and then spend $4.50 when purchasing the second which means it would cost you $.50 overall to set up this trade.

Assume you then hold onto the options until the middle of August, and the option with the August expiration date is fast approaching. At this point in time, the premium on it has dropped substantially so now it only costs $1.50. At this point, the September option still has a month's room to move about, so the premium is holding firm at $3. At this point, you would want to close the spread position. You would purchase the August option back for $1.50 and sell the September option for $3, thus generating a $1.50 profit. Once you subtract the initial $.50 you still have a $1 profit. This technique is as effective for calls as it is for puts.

201

CHAPTER 5: RATIO SPREAD STRATEGY

The ratio spread trading strategy is a variation of the vertical spread strategy which involves an option spread using the same expiration date for multiple strategies. This is a neutral strategy that is useful when it comes to taking advantage of an underlying stock that has an extremely low amount of volatility. Much as the name implies, this strategy works by setting up an opening at a ratio of options sold to the number of options bought. The specific ratio can vary based on your personal needs, though the examples outlined below will deal with a 2 to 1 ratio of options sold to options bought.

Ratio spread strategies are an ideal companion when it comes to stocks that are certified non-volatile. Broadly, they are similar to trading strategies such as the butterfly or the iron condor with one major difference. Specifically, ratio spreads have a greater chance of loss if the underlying stock

202

ends up being too volatile. This risk is then offset due to the fact that these spreads are built using fewer options total which means there will be fewer commission costs related to opening and closing the positions.

Put ratio spread

The put ratio spread has a neutral risk and profit profile that is constructed, unsurprisingly, by using put options. To put it into play you are going to want to purchase one put option that is in the money and sell two more put options that are current for the money. This strategy can be put into play for practically no upfront cost and may actually end up generating a small amount of profit. This occurs because the cost of the in the money option is going to be very close to, or less than, the amount made when selling the two at the money options.

It is important to keep in mind that the put ratio spread will not generate extra losses or profit if the underlying stock price rises above the in the money price of the first put options strike price. This is the case because if this occurs then all of the put options will expire worthlessly. After the price of the underlying stock dips below the in the money strike price, you will be able to earn a profit by selling the in the money option that was previously purchased. This profit will continue to increase as the price of the underlying stock continues to dip.

However, it is also important to keep in mind that once the price of the underlying stock drops below the at the money strike price of the puts you are selling the potential for profit will start to decrease rapidly. At this point, the at the money put options will no longer expire as worthless and must be bought back to prevent additional losses. As this will require you to purchase 2 options while only selling 1 the losses will continue to mount as the price of the underlying stock continues to drop.

As such, the put ratio spread can be thought to have a profit profile that is neutral with a slightly bullish tinge. It can achieve maximum profit only if the underlying stock price ends at the at the money put strike price. When this occurs, you can then sell the in the money put option while letting the other pair expire. Upward volatility will not generate additional profits or losses as all three puts will be affected equally and cancel out the greater profits. Meanwhile, losses due to downward volatility are going to be practically limitless. As such, this strategy should only be used with stocks that are neutral and non-volatile, and you are confident that they will stay this way until the strategy is complete.

Call ratio spread

The call ratio spread strategy uses call options in a variation of the standard vertical spread that uses a ratio of call options, most commonly in a 2:1 format. This is a neutral strategy that is best used on stocks that show a low degree of volatility. To utilize this strategy, you are going to want to purchase one in the money call option while selling a pair of call options that are at the money. As you are selling a greater number of options than you are purchasing, it is important to keep in mind that the additional options are going to be uncovered which makes the potential for loss significant if you choose poorly.

Due to this fact, the call ratio spread is considered a neutral strategy that is only suitable for non-volatile stocks. It creates a scenario where a falling stock price generates little to no losses while gains create the potential for unlimited losses.

Be careful when using them and ensure that there are no news releases forthcoming as this can easily change a low-volatility stock into one with a high level of volatility.

This creates an extra layer of inherent risk with this strategy, and certain brokers will not let you go through with it until you have proved yourself experienced. However, this risk is mitigated to some degree as you have the possibility of earning a profit through the sale as the in the money call option will always be offset by selling the at the money options.

Once the expiration date arrives, if the price of the underlying stock drops below the strike price then all of the options are going to expire without making a profit, though they won't cost you anything extra either. If the underlying stock price ends up being greater than the in the money strike price, then you will be able to sell the option that is in the money for a profit. The amount of income that is generated by this sale will increase the closer the price is to the at the money price of the other options you purchased.

If the price of the underlying stock ends up being greater than the at the money strike price, then you will need to buy back the at the money calls to avoid losing money. As you will need to buy back more options than you are selling this will create an ever-increasing potential for loss. As such, the maximum way to generate a profit with this strategy will see the price of the underlying stock finishing up exactly at the at the money strike price. This will allow you to sell the in the money option for the greatest amount possible while still allowing the at the money calls to expire worthlessly.

CHAPTER 6: FRONT SPREAD STRATEGY

Call front spread

The front spread call strategy allows you to purchase a call that is already in the money, or slightly below the point where it would be on the money, at a discounted price. The end goal is to then gain control of the call at the initial strike price for either a small debit or even a credit through the selling of 2 calls at the second strike price. Both strike prices will need to utilize the same expiration month in order for this strategy to be effective.

When utilizing this strategy, you are going to need to be aware that it has an extremely large risk ceiling. This means you are going to need to use traditional indicators in order to determine if the time is right for this strategy in order to prevent yourself from taking a loss when the underlying asset moves more than you expect it to. This strategy is best used if you are slightly bullish about the underlying asset and you believe it will move to the second strike price and then completely stop. If the strength of the market is in question, utilizing a different strategy is recommended.

In order to achieve maximum results with this strategy, you are going to need the underlying asset price to rise from the first strike price to the second. This, in turn, provides cover for one of the calls you purchase while also leaving the second one open to the potential of even greater profits moving forward. This second call will also leave you open to additional risk if the market turns against you unexpectedly. This means you are going to want to keep a close eye on the movement of the underlying asset to ensure quick movements are countered. You will also want to include a strong stop loss situated just below the second strike point to prevent yourself from losing everything.

You can further mitigate the potential for risk through the use of index options rather than standard options. Index options are always a great choice when it comes to utilizing riskier strategies because they are the least volatile type of option you can purchase. This is due to the fact that the movement of various options in the index typically tends to cancel one another out.

To utilize this strategy, the first thing you will need to do is to purchase a call at the initial strike price. You will then want to follow this purchase up with the sale of a pair of calls that are listed at the secondary strike price. The price of the underlying stock should then ideally move enough that you make a profit from the first option while still being able to sell off the pair of calls to fund most if not all of the purchase.

When utilizing this strategy, you are going to want to keep in mind that that the closer the first call is to the expiration date, the greater your potential for profit is going to be. As such, the timeframe that is typically considered the most effective for this strategy is between 30 and 45 days. You can also utilize this strategy through the purchase of the underlying asset directly as opposed to utilizing uncovered calls which mitigate the potential risk somewhat.

Keep in mind that time decay is working in your favor through the use of this strategy. While it will still reduce the value of the option you plan on purchasing, this loss will ultimately be outweighed by the gain that will come with the pair of options you are going to sell.

Put front spread

The put front spread strategy is best used for the purchase of a put that is just at the money or slightly out of the money while not paying full price in the process. When everything works according to plan, you will be able to purchase the put at the second strike price while still earning credit or just a small debit. This extra profit comes from selling two additional puts at the first strike price.

In order for this strategy to be as effective as possible, you will need the price of the underlying asset to decrease from where it starts at the second strike price all the way to the initial strike price. This means you are going to want to utilize this strategy only when the market is feeling bearish. Additionally, you are only going to want to undertake this strategy when the indicators you favor say that the underlying asset is going to drop in price, but only a small amount. This is extremely important if you are going to come out on top as only one of your puts is covered. As such, if the stock moves dramatically you can potentially see significant losses.

This means it is very important to closely monitor the underlying asset when you utilize this strategy and never do so without having a firm stop loss in place to counter potential losses. Much like the call variation, the optimal time frame for this strategy is between 30 and 45 days from when the option will expire.

In order to utilize this strategy, you are going to want to begin by selling a pair of puts at the initial strike price. Next, you purchase a put at the secondary strike price assuming the price of the underlying asset is going to remain at or above this price.

When using this strategy, you are going to want to try and get the price of the underlying asset to end up as close to the first strike price as possible at the moment the option expires. This will ensure that you make the maximum amount of each trade. The amount of profit that you can make on the trade will be determined by the differences between the two strike prices after any net debits are taken into account. On the other hand, the maximum amount of possible loss can be determined by adding the strike prices together. If the underlying asset drops all the way down, this is what you can expect to lose.

When using this strategy, your goal should be for the implied volatility to decrease as time goes on. Doing so will decrease the value of the options you sold at twice the rate of the options you purchased, netting an overall profit.

CHAPTER 7: BACKSPREAD STRATEGY

Also known as reverse ratio spreads, backspreads are a type of option trading strategy that is best utilized when you feel that a specific underlying stock is going to experience a high degree of volatility and you have a fairly good idea of what direction the price is going to move in but aren't 100 percent convinced. If the underlying stock then moves a large amount in the direction, you predicted you would earn a large profit. If it moves in the opposite direction instead, then you will still earn a profit, though it won't be as large. However, if the underlying stock only moves a small amount, then you will see a loss instead.

Put backspread

If you are bearish on the underlying stock in question, then you are going to want to use what is known as a put backspread, or possibly a put ratio spread as put options are utilized in the strategy. To begin using this strategy, you are going to want to start by purchasing any number of put options that are currently out of the money. At the same time, you are going to want to sell a smaller number of put options that are on the money. The end result here is that you end up with a premium net credit.

While you can use any number of put options for this strategy, the simplest variation is to sell 1 in the money put option and purchase two put options that are currently out of the money. If the underlying stock then moves higher than the strike price of the in the money put option that was sold you can allow it to expire while still holding onto the credit premium as all three put options will now expire worthlessly.

If the stock price finishes up somewhere between the in the money strike price and the strike price of the pair of out of the money options, then you will lose money as you will need to buy back the in the money option and the pair of out of the money options are going to expire. However, if the price of the underlying stock drops lower than the strike price of the out of the money put option you will begin to see potentially unlimited profits as the cost of purchasing the in the money option will be greatly offset by the profits you will make selling the pair of out of the money options.

It is very important to keep in mind the fact that you cannot allow your backspread positions to expire as you will have already sold options that will need to be repurchased in order to prevent them from being exercised. As such, it is important to always ensure you have enough available funds to buy back those options in case the price of the underlying stock doesn't move.

Call backspread

Also known as the call ratio backspread, the call backspread is the type of backspread you are going to want to use if you are bullish on the underlying stock you have your eye on. The call backspread can be done by purchasing any number of out of the money call options and selling a smaller number of call options that are currently on the money. The most common way this is done is by purchasing a pair of out of the money call options and selling one call option that is currently in the money. This strategy will generate a premium as the cost of the two options will be offset by selling the third.

If the price of the underlying stock drops below the strike price, then all three of the options will expire worthlessly. You will still net the initial premium, however. If the underlying stock moves to the point that is higher than the in the money strike price but is still below the strike price of the initial calls, then you are going to lose money as the pair of calls will be worthless but you will still need to buy back the call at the in the money strike price. Once the price of the underlying stock moves past the on the money strike price, then your potential for profit really kicks into high gear. The in the money call will continue to increase in value so will need to be bought back, but this price will be mitigated by the extra gains seen from the pair of calls whose gains will keep pace with it.

CHAPTER 8: TRADING WITH TECHNICAL

INDICATORS

As the name implies, technical indicators are used in options trading as a way to determine trends as well as potential turning points in the price of underlying stocks. When used correctly, they can accurately predict movement cycles as well as determine when the most profitable time to buy or sell is going to be.

Technical indicators are typically calculated based on the price pattern of a derivative or stock. Relevant data includes closing price, opening price, lows, highs and volume. Indicators typically take the data regarding a stock's price from the past few periods depending on the charts the analyst favors and use it to generate a trend that will show what has been happening with a specific stock as well as what is likely to happen next.

Technical indicators tend to come in two main types lagging and leading. Lagging indicators are those which are based on preceding data and help to determine when a trend is forming or if a stock is currently trading in range instead. The stronger the trend the lagging indicator pinpoints, the greater the chance that it is going to continue moving forward. However, lagging indicators are of no use when it comes to determining future rally points or potential pullbacks.

Alternately, leading indicators are useful when it comes to predicting the point where the price of a given stock may rally or crash. These are typically momentum indicators which gauge the momentum of the movement the price of an underlying stock is likely to take. A momentum indicator can be thought of as the common sense that says a ball thrown into the air will not continue in the same direction forever, once it begins to slow you can accurately predict that it will soon begin to move in the opposite direction.

Leading indicators are useful when it comes to determining if the price of an underlying stock has reached an unsustainable point and when likely slowdown of a given price will occur. As stocks that are overbought or oversold are in for a pullback, having this information before the move occurs can be extremely useful when used with numerous trading strategies.

Both types of indicators are equally important as you will need to determine what types of trends are going to be forming as well be on the lookout for eventual slowdowns and pullbacks at any time in order to use many strategies successfully. Typically, you are going to want to use at least three indicators at all times.

Moving Average Convergence Divergence Indicator

The moving average convergence divergence (MACD) indicator is an oscillating indicator that typically moves between a zero point and a centerline. When used, a very high value will indicate that an underlying stock is in danger of being overbought and a consistently low value will show that the stock is oversold.

MACD charts are based on a combination of 3 different exponential moving averages (EMA). These averages can be based on any period, though the most common are the 12-26-9 chart. The first part of this chart is generally listed as the 12-day and 26-day EMA. The 12-day EMA is the faster of the two.

Using a faster and a slower EMA allows you to accurately gauge the momentum of the trend you are following. If the 12-day EMA is above the 26-day EMA, then you can assume the underlying stock is in an uptrend while the reverse is also true. When the 12-day EMA increases at a rate that is much greater than that of the 26-day EMA, then the uptrend is likely to become more pronounced. When the 12-day EMA begins to slow and draws close to the 26-day EMA, then the trend's momentum is going to fade letting you know the uptrend will end soon.

The MACD makes use of these 2 EMAs by looking at the difference between them and plotting that difference. If the 12-day and the 26-day are the same, then the MACD will be 0. If the 12-day is higher than the 26-day, then the MACD will be positive and vice versa. The greater the difference between the pair, the further the MACD line will be from the centerline (if positive) or zero (if negative).

On its own, this line doesn't provide that much more information than a standard moving average. It becomes much more useful when the 9-day EMA is added to the mix. The 9-day EMA is different than the others in that it is the EMA of the MACD line, not of a stock price. This EMA then acts as the other EMA lines and smooths out the MACD line to make its results more manageable.

There is also a more complicated way to use the MACD indicator which is known as the MACD histogram. The histogram can be thought of like the difference between the MACD line and the 9-day EMA. When the MACD line crosses above the 9-day EMA, the MACD histogram will cross above 0 which indicates a bullish signal. If it crosses below 0, then it indicates a bearish trend. When charted, if the histogram forms a series of descending peaks this is known as a negative divergence with a positive divergence being indicated by a series of ascending peaks.

When a negative divergence occurs, it is a sign that the current positive uptrend is likely to reverse sooner than later. This can happen even if the pattern of the underlying stock price itself seems to be moving higher and higher on the chart. The reverse is also true. These signals can become somewhat muddy when the price trades at the range for a prolonged period of time which is why it is important to always use multiple indicators to avoid seeing false signals.

Average directional index

The average directional index acts as a type of guide that confirms the signals generated by other technical indicators you may choose to use. Once a trend is identified, the average directional index can determine its relative strength. The average directional index is a combination of both the positive and negative directional indicators which track upward and downward trends respectively. The average directional index then combines them into a unified way to determine the relative strength of a trend.

The average directional index is an oscillating indicator with a range between 0 and 100. Zero indicates a flat trend with virtual no volatility while 100 indicates that a given stock is moving practically straight up or down with a large degree of volatility. This indicator only measures the relative strength of the trend, it will not tell you which direction it is likely to move in.

In general, you will want to keep in mind that average directional index values rarely reach above 60 as trends of this strength typically only appear in long recession or very long runs when the market is bullish. As such, a value that is greater than 40 can be considered a vibrant trend while a value below 20 means that the underlying stock is in what is known as a trading range.

When it comes to signals that are produced by the average directional index, if a trend moves from above 40 to below then you can deduce that the trend is slowing which is a bad sign for most popular options trading strategies. As such, if you see this movement occur you can assume that it is time to close out your existing positions. On the other hand, if you see a trend move from below 20 to a point somewhere above it then you can assume that the sideways market movement is coming to an end and a new major trend is going to soon be forming. Depending on the direction of the trend you will then be able to decide if you need to adopt a strategy that is bearish or one that is bullish.

Additionally, you can also determine useful information when it comes to the point where the positive directional index and the negative directional index cross paths. When the positive directional index crosses above the negative directional index from below then you can assume the signal is bullish. When the negative directional index crosses above the positive directional index from below then you know that the trend is going to be bearish instead.

Regardless of the strength of the trends, you find it is recommended that you never base your options trade on just one indicator. Ideally, you will want to use at least three in order to confirm the signals you are seeing aren't flukes and to ensure you prevent false alarms.

CHAPTER 9: WEEKLY OPTIONS TRADING

Weekly options are those that are listed for the purpose of providing short-term trading along with ample opportunities for hedging. As the name implies, they expire every week. They are listed on Thursday and expire the next Friday. Weekly options have been around for years but were traditionally only traded by investors working in cash indices. This all changed in 2011 when the number of ways that weekly options could be traded was expanded by the Chicago Board of Options. While at first there were only 28 underlying stocks that qualified to be traded weekly, that number has now grown to over 800.

In addition to their timeframe, weekly options differ from traditional options in other ways as well. There is one week of every month when weekly options are not available. They are also not listed as part of the monthly options expiration style. Technically the week that monthly options expire they are the same as weekly options.

Weekly option advantages

Trading weekly options come with several advantages. First and foremost, purchasing weekly options provides you with the opportunity to buy exactly what you need with less upfront capital required. As such, if you are looking for a swing trade for just a few days or even a day trade, weekly options are the right choice. For sellers, weekly options all you to sell more frequently as opposed to just once per month.

Weekly options trades also allow you to reduce the cost of trades that have a long-term spread including diagonal spreads and calendar spreads because you can then sell weekly options against them. High volume traders can also use weekly options as a way to hedge larger portfolios and positions against the risk that comes along with certain events. When the market at large is range bound, the weekly options market can still be utilized for strategies including the iron condor and butterflies of multiple types.

Weekly option disadvantages

The quick expiration date of weekly options means that you won't have much time for the market to turn around if you make a poor choice. If you are selling options, it is important to be aware that the gamma for them is going to be much more sensitive than with traditional options. As such, if you are shorting options then a small overall move can turn an option that is just out of the money into one which is deep in the money extremely quickly.

Weekly options require much more active risk management. If you do not take the time to properly size your trades and lock your profits, they can drain your trade balance quickly.

Additionally, implied volatility is going to be much higher because of the timeframe as well. Near-term options are always going to be more vulnerable when it comes to dramatic price swings.

Buying weekly calls/puts

As you have a much more limited amount of time to turn a profit, your timing when purchasing a weekly call or put needs to be spot on. If you choose poorly when it comes to price direction, strike selection and timeframe you can easily end up sitting on an option that is completely worthless. You will need to be aware of your level of risk aversion because while the cost is going to be cheaper, you will generally want to purchase a greater number of options each week.

Ideally, you are going to want to avoid naked call or put options with weekly calls as they tend to be low probability trades. If you have a bias towards a specific direction, then a structured trade or a debit spread is often preferable.

Selling weekly calls and puts

Selling weekly options can generate a reliable amount of success in the long term. You are defining your profit margins up front, however, so it is important to have a firm idea of what your options are worth to avoid selling yourself short. Selling weekly trades will allow you to collect the full premium if you guess correctly but exposes you to undefined losses if you choose poorly which requires an extra margin.

The best types of underlying stocks for these trades are lower priced as they each take up a smaller amount of your overall buying power. It is also easier to bet on high implied volatility as it is more likely to revert to the mean in the given timeframe. As a rule, selling a put in the short term is preferable to selling a call as it tends to generate a higher return in the weekly market.

Spreads

Selling an option and purchasing an option that is further in the money is a great way to take advantage of the weekly market. As the overall implied level of volatility is much higher in the weekly market, the spread can help you in case the direction reverses unexpectedly before you have a chance to do anything about it. Selling an option against the long option naturally, reduces the role implied volatility would have on the successful trade. Ideally, you will want to use a debit spread near the point where the current price is sitting and aim for a 1 to 1 trade when it comes to risk and reward.

Butterfly spread

This is an ideal trade to make when the implied volatility is at its maximum. The body of the butterfly benefits from the decrease in implied volatility moving forward while the underlying stays near the short strikes. Buying them is typically going to be more effective as well because you can typically pick them up at the weekly market for what amounts to 0 additional cost or possibly a small debit. This strategy is particularly effective if used just prior to an earnings announcement as you can still earn money from the credit even if you bet on the wrong direction or the trend doesn't extend as far as you expected.

CONCLUSION

Thank you for making it through to the end of *Options Trading: Strategies on How to Excel at Options Trading*, let's hope it was informative and able to provide you with all of the tools you need to achieve your options trading goals, whatever it is that they may be. Just because you've finished this book doesn't mean there is nothing left to learn on the topic, expanding your horizons is the only way to find the mastery you seek.

New option trading strategies and technical indicators are always being developed, and it is important that you continue to seek them out as you never know when you might stumble across a new favorite. Above all else it is important to avoid resting on your laurels as being satisfied with your overall skill level is really just the first step to letting the competition get a leg up on you.

The next step is to stop reading already and to get ready to try out all the strategies you have learned. While many traders may recommend practicing with a dummy account first, a better solution is to practice with low-value trades instead. Practicing with a dummy account doesn't allow you to practice your trading mindset which means that when you get back out into the real world, you will have to deal with potential pitfalls that can turn a strategy that worked quite well with the pretend trades into something of a nightmare when used in the real world.

Take it slow and always take small, reliable returns over the potential of huge, risky windfalls. Never risk more in a given trade than you can afford to lose and before you know it you will be a successful veteran options trader. Remember, successful options trading is a marathon, not a sprint, slow and steady wins the race.

Finally, if you found this book useful in any way, a review on Amazon is always appreciated!

Sign Up & Join <u>Andrew Johnson's Mailing List!</u>

*EXCLUSIVE UPDATES

*FREE BOOKS

*NEW REALEASE ANNOUCEMENTS BEFORE ANYONE ELSE GETS THEM

*DISCOUNTS

*GIVEAWAYS

FOR NOTIFACTIONS OF MY *NEW RELEASES* :

Never miss my next **FREE PROMO**, my next **NEW RELEASE** or a **GIVEAWAY!**